Yah¹
The Blac. ...

By Rabbi Simon Altaf Hakohen

Second Edition
Revision 20, Jul 2014

Rabbi Simon Altaf, email: shimoun63@yahoo.com
Rabbi Lamont Clophus, Forever-Israel, 8111 Mainland, Suite 104-152, San Antonio, Texas, 78240, USA

Rabbi Simon Altaf for African-Israel International Union of Qahalim or please contact us via e-mail through foreverisrael777@yahoo.com or phone Rabbi Kefa in the USA: Tel 1-210-827-3907.

Visit our website at: www.forever-israel.com

All quotes are from the Hidden Truths Hebraic Scrolls formerly called the Abrahamic-Faith Netzarim Hebraic Study Scriptures (HTHS) unless otherwise stated.

Note:

I will be using the term Elohim though the real name of Elohim is YHWH the four sacred letters. The original name of the Messiah is Yahushua and not Jesus or the many variants found around the world which is one more distortion and corruption from the nations around us. The western nations have helped to spread this deception further by endorsing things not heard or seen. For brevity and to make it easier plus the fact I do not know how the sacred name in my book will be handled I will be using more of Elohim rather than YHWH knowing full well it is not wrong to call Him Elohim but that its better not to handle the sacred name especially if one is ritually unclean as many will be who may read this book and may not understand this very important aspect of the Torah.

I will not use 'Jesus' The Western Roman name but the real name of the Messiah Yahushua from the Hebrew. Yeshua the short form is an Aramaic name and not Hebrew either. Aramaic and Hebrew were both languages of my forefathers in Iran from whom I descended a kohenim (Levitical priests) clan. Those who insist on the saviour's name being Yeshua really do not have any understanding of the two Semitic languages. YHWH is my teacher (Ps 119:33) and my guide and He alone is the one who called me out in 1998 and I thank Him alone and all the other people He sent into my life.

All the references in this book will be from the Hidden-Truths Hebraic Study Scrolls publication and where different will be stated as such as the King James Version Bible.

Preface

I was compelled to write this book because the time has come in my ministry where by the revelations that I was given now need to be spoken about. I was given certain revelations about Israel and her future restoration and I will document more of these in my upcoming book World War III – The Final Exodus but here I speak more about their ancestry and lineages. I felt that since Elohim is going to restore everything therefore the rightful place and colour of Messiah is very important for all of us to know. We love Him as our Master and Saviour. We would like to honour His name and esteem him to give him honour and glory rightly due to him.

This book is not about black power, black theology or black politics but this book is about Elohim's chosen race of people and who they are and the Messiah who He actually belongs to.

This book is not an anti-white book or a polemic against white people but nevertheless Elohim used them in His plans to punish our people who went astray from the truth. I use the term white opposed to Caucasian because Cauc-Asians were not pure white races but a mixture of Asians who lived in the Russian steppes.

The white Christ that was conceived by the Roman clergy and later used by Europeans Christians, conquering nations in the guise of taking the gospel to them and what should have been used to FREE people was used to enslave the Africans who were rightly the people of the Bible. The time has now come to correct the wrongs and set forth what is the truth. If we are going to embrace the truth then it better be the whole truth and not just the bits that we like as many have decided to do exactly that in the west. Even the white people need the Saviour Yahushua but in His pure form and with His unadulterated Torah which has been perverted by the Western Clergies who have mixed it with paganism and mistruths.

I belong to the true house of Israel the Shemitic house and not the Khazarian Ashkanazim (European) converts that call themselves Jews today, they occupy the land of Israel which is not their land and neither their inheritance. The Khazari converts identified themselves as the sons of Japheth are none the less

3

occupiers of Israel today for good reasons but it is allowed by YHWH and in His time He will deal with them.

> The 13th Tribe p28 by Arthur Koestller
> Eldad visited Spain around 880 and may or may not have visited the Khazar country. Hasdai briefly mentions him in his letter to Joseph – as if to ask what to make of him. Joseph then proceeds to provide a genealogy of his people. Though a fierce Jewish nationalist, proud of wielding the 'sceptre of Judah", he cannot, and does not, claim for them Semitic descent; he traces their ancestry not to Shem, but to Noakh's third son, Japheth.

The modern converts have no Semitic connections to the land of Israel and are not from the ancient blood-line of the Hebrews. My ancestors were given the land and then later expelled from it for disobedience. My ancestors the true Hebrews were in fact all black and not white however today we have fair white colours through mixing in our families.

I am not going to run to Israel and claim territory that the Zionists took over in 1948 but Elohim in his own time will give us what is rightfully ours. We wait for our Messiah Yahushua to deliver us our rightful inheritance and His kingly rule yet to be revealed to the world. Elohim has taken me back to my real people and connected me with the ancient past and given me wisdom to understand and expound on His Scriptures. When Yahushua called me out of Islam He called me with a mission.

My mission is to establish the law of Elohim, the truth of the Torah for the restoration of our people to prepare for the soon return of our Master and Messiah Yahushua and now revealing the Black Messiah is probably going to be the most important work I have written to date as part of my mission. The much misunderstood New Covenant that HE cut with His disciples for the whole of Israel.

The western world decided to change the image of the Messiah one day from Black to white. Every image of the White Messiah which the Caucasians refer to as 'Jesus' which is presently in the home of any Christian believer is nothing short of an abomination that has traded the truth for a lie. In this book I use His real name

Yahushua and not 'Jesus' because YHWH is restoring everything and the restoration starts with the name, His culture, His people and His true heritage.

Furthermore when we invent a new Messiah and give him a new colour, name and even nationality such as Rome did instead of Him being an Israeli Yahudi then we have invented our own elohim and have gone into idolatry which many churches are living in because they serve the dictates of Rome that says Elohim's law is no more and that this person of 'Jesus' looked white which was used as a sign of oppression for our people. Yes YHWH allowed this for our own sins for the sins of our ancestors but the time has come to repent and to be restored to our past Inheritance.

Gone are the days of slavery when Black men were whipped by the white races using a mfeemboo (Made from hippopotamus hide) and called all sorts of bad names as baboons, monkeys, apes, and four footed animals. This is how they were put down because of the disobedience of our people to Elohim.

The white blondie European 'Jesus' was used to enslave the blacks and to put them down as inferior races while the first man Adam was created from the earth and was fully Black. The whole world descended from one Black man but the Western world loves to paint him with a white skin so the deception still continues. I believe these things were allowed to take place because of the disobedience of genetic Israel (Black people) who were cursed with curses for not believing and behaving right according to Torah. The curses of Torah will lift off immediately the minute genetic Israel repents and returns to Torah and this is happening as we speak.

YHWH has instilled a fire in me and from the very day I took up His offer in 1998 September to follow Him I have a holy fire burning in me, every moment of my life I have YHWH the holy Eloah in my blood and I only want to be in His will. He took me to Africa after eleven years of my conversion in 2010 and there I met some of the real members of the tribes of the Hebrew faith. Many people who see Israel restored in 1948 and occupied by European Jewry do not realize that the majority of these Jews came out of the Khazari kingdom near the Black Sea and a whole nation of Caucasian converts into the Jewish faith.

Today the majority of Ashkenazim Jews are nothing more than European people who are actually the sons of Japheth and not Shem. The real sons of Shem are shunned even in Israel who are the Falasha Yahudi and are treated as third or even fourth class citizens because they are Black Ethiopians. But is that not the attitude of the European and Western people generally against the Blacks so we should not be surprised at this treatment. They became the instrument of judgment.

If we look at the Ethiopian history both Menelick I and Menelick II were the descendants of the real King Solomon the son of King Dawud. The name menelick when broken into its Hebrew is men meaning "from" and melek meaning king so the word menelick means "from the king." Historically the Italians had ambitions to rule parts of Africa why should they be left behind when Britain and France were already there with Portugal and Holland. The Italians did not think about human right violations and the killing of innocents with mustard gas when they recklessly invaded Ethiopia and tried to overtake it. Their spraying of mustard gas on the population was conveniently ignored by Western European nations who were also busy trying to conquer parts of Africa. This mustard gas killed many sons of Tsiyon in their exile in Ethiopia who were both the sons of King Solomon and later migrations of Hebrews to Ethiopia.

> [1]In 1935 there broke out a war between Italy and Ethiopia the outcome of which was Abyssinia or Ethiopia's acceptance of Italian rule. This incident was not a minor one and has been regarded by history to be one of the thorns that led to the outbreak of World War II. It showed how ineffective the League of Nations was when the great powers chose to disregard it to suit their own interests.
>
> Italy had tried to take over Ethiopia from 1890 but failed to do so. Thus in 1934 Abyssinia was one of the few independent states in the African continent that had not come under the colonial rule of any European power. But Italy under the dictatorship was thirsting for an excuse to annex Ethiopia. A border dispute with Somaliland (under

---

[1] http://www.warchat.org/history/history-world/second-italo-abyssinian-war-1935-1936

Italian control) gave the pretext. Ignoring all pleas Italy marched into Ethiopia on 3rd October 1935.

The Ethiopian army was ill equipped and hardly had any training. Under the onslaught of the Italian Generals Graziani and Badoglio they were relentlessly pushed back and suffered a heavy defeat near Lake Ashangi on 9th April 1936. The capital, Addis Ababa, fell on 5th May. Haile Selassie, the Emperor of Ethiopia fled into exile. From Rome Mussolini declared Victor Emmanuel III to be the new Emperor of Abyssinia? Badoglio was to depute for him as his viceroy.

Ethiopia appealed to the League of Nations, which condemned this invasion by Italy. The League voted to impose economic sanctions on the aggressing country. But it remained only on paper because there was a general lack of support. Britain had interests in East Africa but the other major European powers were indifferent to the plight of an African nation. Italian action was not condoned but nobody was willing to do anything about it. Thus Italy and its imperialistic ambitions got encouraged and ultimately contributed to the escalation of tensions leading to the second Great War.

Haile Selassie the king of Ethiopia a peaceful man was powerless to stop the Italians and on top of this the fact that the Italians used mustard gas to kill his people which caused the Emperor to go to the League of Nations for help who refused to do anything other than condemn the action verbally. Countries such as Holland and her queen said the action was justified. Well then YHWH gave Europe the World War II and that ravaged Europe, the same people who killed his sons and daughters in Ethiopia were now crying the bitter cries that King Haile was originally.

Word war II was a punishment upon the nations by YHWH because of their ill treatment of His people and any time such a thing that will happen in history YHWH will act even if men will remain silent. YHWH is our maker and we have a covenant with Him and He will honour the covenant.

Now coming back to the European Jewry, they are not the real progenitors of the Biblical faith but are certainly converts into Judaism today. Some of these went astray with the heresy of the ancient Karaites who refused any oral instruction of Torah and proclaiming the written Torah while ignoring how to obey the instructions which had to be orally communicated by Moses. Today Christians foolishly think these are the original progenitors of the faith when it is clear that they were not. The ancient Sadducees were the ruling class in the first century Temple and the persecutors of Yahushua and His disciples and the House of Ananus were also the murderers of Jacob the half brother of Yahushua in 62 CE.

It should also be noted that the Hebrews never called themselves Jews in ancient times and is a modern word. The term Jew and Israel are not synonymous. The Hebrews were simply known as Israelites. The term Jews is often misapplied today to the ancient people. The only one tribe that could have the term Yahudi applied still cannot be called by a modern racist word that was coined by the nations against European Jewry.

So being a serious scholar and my heart intent on the complete restoration of my people this book is about the real Messiah and to put Him where He belongs. Africans, its time for you to experience the real Yahushua and not the one given to you by the western Church which was the agenda of the European nations to enslave you in which they largely succeeded but it was also your own fault in that you left the love of YHWH and traded it in for worthless lies in your life and thus ended up wandering like Qayin. Now the time of your wanderings is over and the time of your restoration has come so be ready to embrace the Torah/LAW of Ha'Shem once again that the days of your joy may come through our real Messiah Yahushua. Don't delay the Tikkun (repair of the breech) and turn away from sinfulness and evil works of the flesh.

YHWH loves you and He only requires one thing of you in whichever nation you are in now that you repent and forsake wickedness and to serve Him with a pure heart. Can you do that? That involves obeying the Torah and not religions of the gentiels. Then start a national repentance (repentance means to turn back to Torah not grovelling for forgiveness as gentile religions teach) so that times of healing and joy may return both to your lands and into your lives and the restoration may be completed to take you back to the land of our forefathers Abraham, Isaac and Jacob who were African men and not Europeans.

> **Second Chronicles 7:14** If my people, which are called by my name, shall humble themselves, and **pray, and seek my face, and turn from their wicked ways**; then will I **hear from shamayim (heavens), and will forgive their sin, and will heal their land**.

The slavery as you know was the direct result of the disobedience of YHWH's people and the only way to reverse the curses is to come out of the world's slavery, which be achieved by repenting and asking YHWH to restore you back to His Torah and Messiah. The moment you bring national repentance into your lives and countries I am certain YHWH will act in your favour and start to unfold his final plan for your lives to restore you. He will remove all the devourers that are devouring your lands today of which are predominantly the Western nations. He is waiting for you and your right-ruling leaders to take the first step and gather the people to repent. It's not too hard, now that you have suffered so much you should see that to be healed is easier when you submit before the Creator. The Black Messiah Yahushua came so that He may restore you to your Father in heaven and finally you to your land and Inheritance.

Table of Contents

Chapter 1
What's in a name?

This is the common Christian argument what's in a name. They say we can call YHWH by any name we like its OK, He will understand since He is the creator. I accept that He is the creator and has all the understanding, patience and tolerance that many of us do not have but the name is important. He does not give a name just because men can pervert it and then use whatever they like. A name in Hebrew culture and in African/Asiatic worldview is the person's identity e.g. Israel the name of Isaac's son is today the identity of the nation of Israel. So if I accept the fickle argument what's in a name then according to Eastern culture and customs without a name you have nothing, no tribal lineage, no inheritance and you are nothing but a refugee because everything is defined by what name you are called. The western people who are far removed from the Eastern culture and speak in such disrespect and ignorance need to learn and re-educate themselves that NAME does matter and without a NAME there is no identity or belonging.

The invention of the title 'Jesus' happened just after 1611 when the King James Version Bible was released because the Letter J was not yet invented and most J sounds in the Bible were pronounced using the letter I. The clear distinction between the letter I and J happened in 1634 when an English book was written that distinguished the letter J and the letter I.

As soon as the letter J was brought into the new vocabulary every translation of the bible subsequently started to refer to the person of Yahushua as 'Jesus.'

This was approximately 376 years ago and before the first printing of the King James Version bible in 1611 we do not find the letter J in the English language hence therefore before this the title 'Jesus' was referred to as Iesous. The first part of the restoration in our life requires and mandates that we restore the name back both of Elohim and Yahushua.

Here is a quote from a King James Version Bible the original 1611 edition.

Matthew 1:1, 25
CHAP. I. 1 The genealogie of Christ from Abraham to Ioseph. 25 And knewe her not, till shee had brought forth her first borne sonne, and he called his name IESVS.

Note in the 1611 version in the King James Bible there is no letter J but it was common practice to use the letter I instead to pronounce the name as Iesous. This pronunciation started early on after the gospels that were written in Hebrew were translated into the Greek language.

From this time on the Christian church has been propagating the myth that the gospels were written in Greek while no such thing happened. They say a lie said enough times might then appear to be true. In fact the custom to write sacred writings in Israel was always in the native Hebrew language. If today you ask any Christian scholar they start parroting with their 24,000 manuscripts of the Greek New Testament but these same scholars have no idea of the 15,000 manuscripts of the Aramaic New Testament that are held by various people of the east. According to Josephus the Jewish historian the son of Yosef of Arimathaea (See Beyth Yahushua www.african-israel.com) he said that very few Yahudim understood the Greek language (Antiquities XX, XI 2) yet we are led to believe that the majority of the NT was in the Greek language.

YHWH made a covenant with the Hebrew people in the language of Hebrew or do you want to believe that Moses also spoke Greek!!! The laughter continues but the time has now come to know truth and to come out of all sorts of paganism and ill beliefs parading as truth. This is to be expected when people instead of examining history and facts rely on third hand scholars who simply have taken the information from others before them and parrot the same so called truth which is not.

One has to ask one question to bring this who fable down. What language did Judah speak? Well the language of Judea, Nazareth and other areas of Israel was Hebrew however with different dialects (Matt 26:73). Elohim would not be sending a Messiah speaking Greek to a Hebrew speaking Yahudim. We know the language of the land was indeed Hebrew hence why Pilate would have the inscription in Hebrew also.

Just because Mel Gibson believes or puts on a movie depicting the story of a German Nun Sister Anne Emmerich from the 18th century which is mixed truth adding to it the Roman theology to confuse the narrative of the Bible with the real story of Yahushua.

What Mel Gibson showed on Screens was definitely not accurate truth of the writings of the Netzarim. In fact his story was fairly inaccurate but I find many Christians gullible who were not able to make the distinction by picking up their bibles and looking for themselves. In fact while Mel is a Catholic and Christians usually hold quite strong views about the Catholics but this time around they forgot that you cannot use a corrupted story to preach truth which many Christians were unwisely promoting his film of half truths.

Here is proof Yahushua spoke Hebrew instead of what is shown in the film…

> **Luke 4:17** And there was delivered to him the scroll of the prophet Yeshayahu (Isaiah).

Yahushua was given the book of Isaiah to read for the Haftorah reading so what was the language of the book of Isaiah? **It was in Hebrew and not Aramaic.** The Haftorah reading would have been done in the Hebrew language as was custom and law in the land of Israel. However the Western scholars without any knowledge of local custom insist that they spoke Greek which is clearly without proof.

> **Luke 4:4** And Yahushua answered him, saying, it is written, that man shall not live by Lechem (bread) alone.

Yahushua once again spoke Hebrew and gave this verse to the devil from the fifth book of the law of Elohim, Deuteronomy 8:3 which was in Hebrew.

> **Luke 23:38** And a superscription also was written over him in letters of Greek, and Latin, and Hebrew, THIS IS THE KING OF THE YAHUDIM.

This is clear proof that the book of Luke was also written in Hebrew by a Hebrew speaking Yahudi called Luka, see my book Beyth Yahushua for his identity.

The question should be since no one in Israel according to the scholars spoke Hebrew then would you not think that the inscription in Hebrew would be redundant and why was it not Aramaic? The Greek and Latin were for the Romans and Greek people while the Hebrew was for the Yahudim who spoke Hebrew extensively.

Here is more proof of Hebrew speeches.

> **Acts 21:40** And when he had given him permission, Rabbi Paulos (Sha'ul) stood on the stairs, and gestured with the hand to the people. And when they had become silent, he spoke to them in the Hebrew language, saying,

Even Rabbi Paulos who was brought up in Tarsus spoke Hebrew fluently.

> **Acts 26:14** And when we were all fallen to the earth, I heard a voice speaking to me, and saying in the Hebrew language, Sha'ul, Sha'ul,

Here is another instance where Yahushua spoke to Rabbi Paulos in Hebrew. Why would he speak to him Hebrew if Rabbi Sha'ul could only speak Greek? Now we can be certain the gospels and in fact the whole Renewed Covenant (NT) was written in Hebrew. In Israel it was an agreed custom to write all the documents that pertain to revelation in Hebrew. So these books likewise would have been written in Hebrew the language of Yahushua. They were able to speak both languages fluently the Hebrew and Aramaic but mixed them to speak at times. Once we remove the myth that Yahushua's disciples wrote the gospels in Greek then we can see through the fog that His name was not 'Jesus' and He communicated fluently in Hebrew.

Chapter 2
Hebrew Israelites - What colour was Moses?

Why do we ask this question? This is because we have some fundamental truths that are told to us in the Torah and one such truth is as follows that a prophet shall come from the midst of Israel speaking with Elohim LIKE UNTO YOU.

> **Deut 18:18** I will raise them up a Prophet from among their brethren, like unto you, and will put my words in his mouth; and he shall speak unto them all that I shall command him.

Why would Elohim say **LIKE UNTO YOU**? This is because like Moses spoke Hebrew so did Yahushua. Like the colour of Moses so would be Yahushua. Then we have to ask what colour was Moses? Let us examine this first.

> **Exodus 2:5-6** And the daughter of Pharaoh came down to wash herself at the river; and her maidens walked along the river's side; and when she saw the ark among the reeds, she sent her maid to get it. **6** And when she had opened it, she saw the child: and, behold, the baby wept. And she had compassion on him and said this is one of the Abrahuan (Hebrews) children.

In order for Pharaoh's daughter to take Moses in to the palace of Pharaoh and not be discovered for forty years he has to be the same colour as the Pharaoh and his daughter who were both of black colour. For forty years Pharaoh believed that Moses was his grandson so think about this. Egypt's Pharaoh's were black and not white. The word for Egypt in Hebrew is Mitzrayim which literally means burnt face (Black) from its ancient root words Kmt. Let us examine this a little for those who challenge that Mitzrayim does not mean burnt face.

Egypt had many names in the past but the name that we use today for Egypt is derived from the Greeks from Aigyptus since they had trouble pronouncing one of the names Egypt was associated with at the time called Het-ka-ptah, which referred to the Temple of Ka for Ptah that they worshipped during that time.

The ancient term for Egypt was KMT pronounced Kemet, which simply means "*THE LAND OF THE BLACKS*", pointing to the rich soil of the Nile valley. What about the Bible term for the son of Noakh called Ham, in Hebrew it is Kham, which has the modern Hebrew letters of חם which means Hot. Not the wording of Kmt and Khm in Hebrew they are identical words that represented the colouring of the nation of Egyptians.

Now anything that remains hot for a significant period of time does not remain white in colour but will eventually turn black so the meaning is implied within the letters Kmt. You can test it and look at your gas burner and see the colour it is. It won't remain of a neutral or clear colour but will be black.

In the most ancient Hebrew hieroglyph it is believed to be as follows: 𐤌 𐤇. It has the picture of waters and a fence. In its ancient meaning it means dark water. However it actually is the following:

Why are these picture important. Hebrew was a monosyllable language in its ancient form and like the Egyptian script shared common characteristics with it. The arms for the letter khet describe the colour Black, Darkness and concealment. All three are evident in the Black Hebrew people today. Many do not know that they are the true Hebrews and run around as Muslims or Christians they are Black and are concealed until the End-Times which is now beginning to unfold. The Mem is the container of water which not only describes water but dark people contained in a land chosen by YHWH.

Now you may understand why the Egyptian word Mitzrayim or in its singular form Mitzri even today in the Arabic language is Misr which simply means country in the Arabic tongue. The Egyptians today refer to their nation as Junhuriyah Misr al-Arabiyah meaning the Arab Republic of Misr (Egypt). Moses was described as a Mitzri (Exodus 2:19) which clearly shows he was Black or identified as a black man from the land (country) of the blacks. Even Rabbi Paulos was identified as an Egyptian in the New Covenant writings then that would also make his colour black (Acts 21:38) and not white as depicted on popular titles.

This is the designation of Egyptians. They are kemetic people which means black. So this shows us that Moses was black in order to survive in the Pharaoh's household. What do you think would happen if he was white? He would be discovered very quickly and you can be certain that he would have been killed and removed from the palace of the Pharaoh. However people do not consider that this is a very important aspect of truth that tells us Moses's colour and ethnicity as a North African.

> **Exodus 2:19** And they said, A Mitzri (Egyptian) delivered us from the hand of the shepherds, and he also drew enough mayim (water) for us, and watered the flock.

Reu'el's daughters looked at Moses and he looked like any other Egyptian, jet black in colour so they said a Mitzri saved us. Moses was of black colour they did not say a white African saved us for they could have said he was laban (white). However when scripture tells us Mitzri it means black face of the country of the blacks. So now you go and examine what colour were ancient Egyptians? As explained they were not white, while the modern Egyptians are much different in colour to their ancient counterparts and a people that actually migrated into the land much later from the East.

> **Acts 21:38** Then you are <u>not that Egyptian</u>, who started a rebellion, and led out into the wilderness four thousand men that were assassins?

> **Exodus 3:6** Furthermore YHWH said to him now put your hand in your bosom. And he put <u>his hand in his bosom: and when he took it out, behold, his hand was leprous, like snow.</u>

Moses when asked by Elohim to put his hand in his bosom the black skin of his hand became white. It would be a notable miracle for him to see his hand changing colour from Black to White.

If Moses was white it would be no miracle to see his hand turned white since he was already white according to the modernist church ideology of what Moses looked like. One thing also we need to understand is that the land of Egypt was called the "Land of the Blacks," which encompassed Ethiopia and Sudan including parts of West Africa. There was no such thing as white men living in Africa. Now one of the famous descendants of Moses was also black namely King David. Many at this point are incredulous to the point of how can that be. Just because you have seen pictures of King David as white, does not make him so. The lies need to stop here and we need to take a truth pill.

Two of King David's ancestors Ruth and Boaz were black. Ruth an Israelite lived in Moab an area occupied by black races the sons of Esav. Boaz lived in Israel which was the area of North Africa and once again an area of blacks. King Solomon was black because both Bathsheba his mother and his father were black. If one was black say the mother then King Solomon may not carry the recessive genes of the mother but the dominant genes of the father. So if we assume the father was white then the baby would have had to be of white hue but in this case he was not which is proof that his father King David was also black.

> **Song of Songs 5:11** His head is as the most pure gold, his locks are curly, and black as a raven.

Only Black people have locks. White people do not have locks no matter how long their hair is.

Bathsheba the mother of King Solomon was black as she was the daughter of Sheba (Gen 10:7, 28, 25:2) (Sudanese and Ethiopians). Note that her first husband was a Uri'yah the Hittite who was a convert into Yahudiot (Judaism) and her father is mentioned as Eliam in Second Samuel 11:3. These were converts into the true faith. Note the modern meaning for Bathsheba is daughter of an oath but that is not the ancient meaning. In its simplest meaning it means the daughter of Sheba which gives us her lineage directly back to Sheba the son of Cush who produced many Nilotic black people.

So both parents would have had to be black in order for King Solomon to be black.

> **First Samuel 17:42** (KJV) And when the Philistine looked about, and saw Dawud, he disdained him: for he was but a

youth, and <u>ruddy</u>, and of a fair countenance.

So how do we deal with the fact that King David is called ruddy? The Hebrew word used to describe as red is the Strong's Admonee (H132). The word more accurately renders the word to mean reddish-black and not red per se.

> **First Samuel 17:42** (HTHS) And when the Philistine looked about, and saw Dawud, he disdained him: for he was but a youth, and reddish-black,[2] and of pleasant looks.

The ancients saw this as the fertile Nile soil which was **reddish black** and nothing to do with the colour of blood which is wrongly assumed. The same principle can be found in the Torah in Genesis 4:10.

> **Beresheeth (Gen) 4:10** (KJV) And he said, What have you done? The voice of your brother's blood (Dam) cries to me from the ground (Adamah).

We can see here that the word play for blood (Dam) and earth (Adamah) is applied which simply sees his life force spilt into the ground, his blood mixed into the earth so it became red-black what is described as the colour of King David.

King David is not being described as white with red complexion that is only the distortion of the European clergy otherwise the Hebrew word Laban would be used, which is found in Genesis 24:49, the man who is described as Rebecca's brother. He would be an Albino though still African. Africa did have her Albinos and also had mulattoes mix of white and black who looked white for all practical purposes.

When YHWH sent leprosy as a judgement it was described as Laban (white). Just by switching words around we cannot make black people white unless they are albinos such as Rebecca's brother Laban was an albino. The plague described in Leviticus 13:4 shows the skin to turn **white** for which the Hebrew word **Laban** is used so be careful how you apply the word and do not

---

[2] Many Africans have this reddish hue to their complexion.

get deceived by cheap doctrines out there as the majority of Hebrew Israelites were black and are still black in the lands of Africa and Asia. Malcolm X was mahogany coloured and his nickname was red based on his appearance of mahogany. If you look at some ancient Egyptian photos you will find they are painted using a red hue depicted as mahogany. So we know King Dawud was black but with a mahogany look (reddish) that is why he is called ruddy and not because he has pale white skin. This is unfortunately the product of unlearned minds.

Night and Day reveals a binary distinction

> **Genesis 1:5** So the evening and the morning were Yom Akhad (Day one).

What YHWH has hidden in the night and day narrative is not just that the day begins in the evening but He has revealed to us a binary distinction such as man/woman, hot, cold, black/white love/hate etc, etc. In actual fact the waters in Genesis though literal but at the drash (allegorical) level are nations. The history of nations began with darkness (black people) because Adam was black so this reveals to us that early history of man would be dominated with the black people as rulers and kings and we see this noting as Adam was the progenitor of all men. We then see that after the darkness period is over the daylight period comes so therefore at a certain time in history we see a switch from black rulers to white rulers which reveals to us the pattern of the night and day we are in the <u>day</u> period of the twenty-four hour cycle right now heading fast towards a close of the day and beginning of the coming era or the messianic day starting with Black again when we are revealed that Black Hebrew Israelites would repent and be restored back to Israel.

The Messiah is black so we head back to start the day with darkness with our dark Messiah. The problem is people have adopted to see the night as a bad thing but it is not. Without the night there is no start to a day. The Black people have been a very important part of our history to give us architecture, governance, science, writing and many other things but unfortunately such things are hidden from modern people for deliberate biases of nations. Even the humble computer was helped to be invented by a black man whose name is forgotten in

20

history. Without his contribution we would not have the present architecture. His name was Dr. Mark Dean.

[3]"America's High Tech "Invisible Man"
By Tyrone D. Taborn

You may not have heard of Dr. Mark Dean. And you aren't alone. But almost everything in your life has been affected by his work.

See, Dr. Mark Dean is a Ph.D. from Stanford University. He is in the National Hall of Inventors. He has more than 30 patents pending. He is a vice president with IBM. Oh, yeah. And he is also the architect of the modern-day personal computer. Dr. Dean holds three of the original nine patents on the computer that all PCs are based upon. And, Dr. Mark Dean is an African American.

So how is it that we can celebrate the 20th anniversary of the IBM personal computer without reading or hearing a single word about him? Given all of the pressure mass media are under about negative portrayals of African Americans on television and in print, you would think it would be a slam dunk to highlight someone like Dr. Dean.

Somehow, though, we have managed to miss the shot. History is cruel when it comes to telling the stories of African Americans. Dr. Dean isn't the first Black inventor to be overlooked Consider John Stanard, inventor of the refrigerator, George Sampson, creator of the clothes dryer, Alexander Miles and his elevator, Lewis Latimer and the electric lamp. All of these inventors share two things:

One, they changed the landscape of our society; and, two, society relegated them to the footnotes of history. Hopefully, Dr. Mark Dean won't go away as quietly as they did. He certainly shouldn't. Dr. Dean helped start a Digital Revolution that created people like Microsoft's Bill Gates and Dell Computer's Michael Dell. Millions of jobs in

---

[3] http://blackjesus.blogs.com/

information technology can be traced back directly to Dr. Dean.

More important, stories like Dr. Mark Dean's should serve as inspiration for African-American children. Already victims of the "Digital Divide" and failing school systems, young, Black kids might embrace technology with more enthusiasm if they knew someone like Dr. Dean already was leading the way.

Although technically Dr. Dean can't be credited with creating the computer that is left to Alan Turing, a pioneering 20th-century English mathematician widely considered to be the father of modern computer science. Dr. Dean rightly deserves to take a bow for the machine we use today. The computer really wasn't practical for home or small business use until he came along, leading a team that developed the interior architecture (ISA systems bus) that enables multiple devices, such as modems and printers, to be connected to personal computers.

In other words, because of Dr. Dean, the PC became a part of our daily lives. For most of us, changing the face of society would have been enough. But not for Dr. Dean, still in his early forties, he had a lot of inventing left in him.

He recently made history again by leading the design team responsible for creating the first 1-gigahertz processor chip... It's just another huge step in making computers faster and smaller. As the world congratulates itself for the new Digital age brought on by the personal computer, we need to guarantee that the African-American story is part of the hoopla surrounding the most stunning technological advance the world has ever seen. We cannot afford to let Dr. Mark Dean become a footnote in history. He is well worth his own history book.

This is not an exhaustive list but we need to know that the black people have patented many inventions but sadly they are never mentioned and others are raised up instead.

Unfortunately because of the sins of the Hebrew Israelites (Black people) YHWH was going to punish them and indeed He did so much so that even their inventions are forgotten and not spoken about while everyone knows about Thomas Edison the inventor of the light bulb but most don't know that the glass was invented by the Black people. While many people give him credit but forget that without the glass there would be no invention of the light bulb. So how many give credit to the Blacks for the glass? Black intelligent people have produced amazing architecture in the ancient times, the pyramids as one such example but rarely do we stop and think of the things we take for granted today such as writing, dwellings, ancient shipping had Blacks at the forefront for these inventions.

Coming back to the issue of darkness we can understand that there are many hidden secrets in the Scriptures, one such secret is that YHWH dwells in darkness. Why would that be?

Second Samuel 22:12 And he made <u>darkness</u> pavilions round about him, dark waters, and thick clouds of the skies.

What does this reveal to us? We look at the drash (allegory) of this verse. It reveals that Elohim had revealed His earlier knowledge about himself to dark people i.e. black people which are referenced in the verse as dark waters (Hebrews). Waters is a symbol of nations so dark waters reveal the early history of man which was to be dominated with black races who were indeed brilliant kings, statesman and legislators.

Africans knew how to run real democratic governments while today's democracy in the west is a sham not worth talking about and are really what one may call police states with cameras watching your every move, spying on your telephone conversations and monitoring your e-mail and internet activity. The allusion of democracy exists in the west but most of these states are spying on their citizens. If you leak any secret of the government then you are in real trouble such as the Wikileaks founder Julian Assange found himself who was being hunted down with false charges by the US government for releasing their confidential data which was not very palatable of what the US has been doing behind closed doors. He was falsely imprisoned with trumped up charges of indecent assault.In turn instead of putting criminal charges on Bankers who wrecked the economy with the credit crunch they were given more handouts and the public were charged tax money to pay for their mistakes. This should show us that the democracy in the West has a long way to go to become a real democracy.

While in the African democratic model the king owned all the land but not for himself but to protect it for the people and his duty was that no one was wronged. His control was primarily to protect the interests of the people so he was a supervisory king, he was not to usurp taxes from the people while in our modern misconstrued model of democracy the leaders become richer and the people poorer and they continually find clever ways o tax people. These things were unheard of in the African democratic model. The model that Africans adopted was taken from the Bible because the Bible is a story of Africa and its people. Abraham and his ancestors were Africans. Yahushua was also North African and black. He was not the white blonde blue eyed as depicted in popular moves and theatres. King Solomon was also of dark black complexion.

It may surprise you to learn that the Africans were people who believed in one Elohim. Akhenaton one ruler of Egypt believed in one Elohim, he taught love, he wrote beautiful poetry just like King David did and he lived one thousand years before him. He banned all paganism in Egypt and banned the priests of Ra. He was king during the time of the children of Israel's sojourn there.

The term dark is not negative and not bad in any sense because one needs to understand it is a part of the twenty-four hour cycle of the day. We do not get 12 hours of our day bad and 12 hours of our day good so it would be wrong to say that the dark part of the day is bad and light part is good. In so far as when it is dark most of the world goes to sleep and it is then that we are refreshed in our bodies while in the light part of the day we expel our energies doing the various vocations we may perform. What then do we learn?

We learn that just as ancient historical rulers had some great and mighty names of black kings and even queens such as Imhotep (2980 BC) who was really the man who invented medicine and surgery which was then later passed to the Greeks who are remembered today but the real man was forgotten. He was even worshipped as a deity by many people including some early Christians after that man's death as a type of Messiah. While the Greeks take credit for everything they did not invent.

Imhotep (2980 BC)
[4]It is Imhotep says Sir William Osler, who was the real Father of Medicine. "The first figure of a physician to stand out clearly from the mists of antiquity." Imhotep diagnosed and treated over 200 diseases, 15 diseases of the abdomen, 11 of the bladder, 10 of the rectum, 29 of the eyes, and 18 of the skin, hair, nails and tongue. Imhotep treated tuberculosis, gallstones, appendicitis, gout and arthritis. He also performed surgery and practiced some dentistry. Imhotep extracted medicine from plants. He also knew the position and function of the vital organs and circulation of the blood system. The Encyclopedia Britannica says, "The evidence afforded by Egyptian and Greek texts support the view that Imhotep's reputation was very respected in early times...His prestige increased with the lapse of centuries and his temples in Greek times were the centers of medical teachings."

Ann Nzinga "Queen of Ndongo" (1582-1663 CE)
In the sixteenth century, the Portuguese stake in the slave trade was threatened by England and France. This caused the Portuguese to transfer their slave-trading activities southward to the Congo and South West Africa. Their most stubborn opposition, as they entered the final phase of the conquest of Angola, came from a queen who was a great head of state, and a military leader with few peers in her time.

The important facts about her life are outlined by Professor Glasgow of Bowie, Maryland:

Queen Hatshepsut (1500 BC)
About 1500 years before the birth of Christ, one finds the beginning of Hatshepsut's reign as one of the brightest in

---

[4] http://www.africanholocaust.net/africanlegends.htm#h

Egyptian history, proving that a woman can be a strong and effective ruler. She was according to Egyptologist, James Henry Breasted, "The first great woman in history of whom we are informed."

Her father, Thothmes I, was highly impressed with the efficiency of his daughter, and appointed her manager, and co-ruler of his kingdom.

Before the King died, he married Hatshepsut to her half-brother, Thothmes II. His reign lasted only thirteen years. After his death, Hatshepsut was to rule only in the name of Thothmes III, until he was old enough to rule alone. Hatshepsut was not satisfied to rule in the name of Thothmes III.

Akhenaton (1375-1358 B.C.)
Amenhotep IV, better known as "Akhenaton, the Heretic King," is in some respects, the most remarkable of the Pharaohs. The account of Akhenaton is not complete without the story of his beautiful wife, Nefertiti. Some archaeologist have referred to Nefertiti as Akhenaton's sister, some have said they were cousins. What is known is that the relationship between Akhenaton and Nefertiti was one of history's first well-known love stories.

Hannibal of Carthage (247-183 B.C.)
Hannibal is said to be the greatest military leader and strategist of all time. Hannibal was born in 247 B.C., when Carthage, then the maritime power, was beginning to decline. The Carthaginians civilisation was a mix of African and Phoenicians, who were great merchants. They traded with India and the people of the Mediterranean, and the Scilly Isles.

When very young, Hannibal accompanied Hamilclar, his father in a battle with the Romans. Seventeen years later, he succeeded his father and became supreme commander of the peninsula. Hannibal had 80,000 infantry, 12,000 cavalry, and 40 African war elephants. He conquered major portions of Spain and France, and all of Italy, except for Rome.

Hannibal marched his army and war elephants through the Alps to surprise and conquer his enemies. In one battle, the Romans put 80,000 men on the field to defeat Hannibal, led by Scipio. When Scipio attacked with his entire army, Hannibal had so studied the grounds and arranged his men so that they surrounded the Romans. He then turned his armoured war elephants loose and trampled them. Behind them, he sent his African swordsmen to complete the slaughter.

In another battle, Rome sent 90,000 men led by Varro and Emilius. With only 50,000 men, knowing he could not win by using his main force, Hannibal placed the weakest part of his army in the center, contrary to the best military rules. With his veterans and cavalry on both wings, the Romans struck them in full center as Hannibal had anticipated. When they were sure of victory by overcoming the center, Hannibal's flank closed in and killed 70,000 men, 80 senators and Emilius.

Hannibal later went on to become a statesman of Carthage, and later took his own life, rather than surrender to Rome.

The list is endless but just to show you that many African forged real history which has been shrouded by many modern historians and even erased to make the black people inferior.

However at the scriptural level this would point to one thing that the binary distinction can be seen by the age starting with black (night) and ending with (white) who will bring the world into destruction and close of history. The white races have been the most destructive. In modern times the financial crisis that we seem to be facing one after another has Caucasians who have masterminded them. This is not so much to lay blame upon them but to show that the modern age will be brought to a close by YHWH by their actions. Then when the new age of Messiah starts it will start with laylah (night) meaning the new day starts with black rule which will be restored throughout Africa and Israel will once again have a black king. No, not just the Messiah but both King David and the Messiah. King David was a black king not white as popularly depicted. Most of Christianities images are incorrect that have been made in modern times.

> **First Kings 8:12** Then spoke Sulahmon, YHWH said that he would dwell in the thick darkness.

> **Psalm 18:9-11** He bowed the shamayim (heavens) also, and came down: and darkness was under his feet. **10** And he rode upon a cherub, and did fly: yes, he did glide upon the wings of the wind.**11** He made darkness his secret place; his pavilions round about him were dark waters and thick clouds of the skies.

YHWH clearly revealed himself that when he descends he would be seen as a dark person meaning black. He has blackness encompassing him all the time because He hides in darkness. So the people who claim to have seen a white 'Jesus' are simply telling fables since no white 'Jesus' exists. Yes a black Yahushua indeed if one can see and find Him.

In Psalm 18:11 the dark pavilions allegorically are his angels who are also of dark features but covered in light. Once again the Western culture has bombarded people with white angels which are imaginations of people but not according to scripture and hidden allegory of YHWH.

Many Atheists run off with this statement that is Elohim dark or light since in other verses it says he is the Father of lights or dwelling in light.

> **James (Jacob) 1:17**... from the Abbah of lights...

> **First Timothy 6:16** Who only has immortality, dwelling in the light which no man can approach to; whom no man has seen, nor can see: to whom be honour and power everlasting. Amein.

Are then these verses of darkness contradictory with the verses of light? No. Both are true. Scripture does not say Elohim is created from light. It says two things one darkness is under his feet or darkness is around his feet and he is the Abbah of lights. Both are true and reflect the binary distinction within YHWH.

28

Yahushua being the image (personality) and glory of Abbah YHWH is black but dwelling in light, so one can see the verses do not contradict each other and this is not a theological statement to argue over. There are practically hundreds of places where these things are revealed in scripture but either in allegory or hidden form yet we do not grasp it because we as humans have our minds fixed on the things of this earth and things we hear, see and perceive. The word for black or darkness in the Hebrew is khoshek and is used 23 times in the book of Iyob (Job) alone where YHWH had a detailed conversation with Iyob.

Elohim showed both His sides during the judgment of Egypt where one side was completely dark and the other light where the Hebrews dwelt.

> **Exodus 10:22-23** And Musa (Moses) stretched out his hand toward shamayim (heavens); and there was <u>thick darkness</u> in all the land of Mitzrayim (Egypt) three days: **23** They did not see one another, nor did anyone rise from his place for three days: but all the children of Y'sra'el had light in their dwellings.

One might construe that the Israelites had light bulbs in their homes but this is not what the Torah is teaching. In fact it shows us the two sides of the coin or what I term binary distinction of YHWH. One side is darkness and the other is light. When we remove the biases in our mind of seeing darkness as a type of evil it is only then that we begin to process and perceive things accurately.

Here YHWH has revealed His kingdom upon Egypt through the darkness. It is simply the absence of light. Both sides allowing us to understand the binary distinction of light/darkness as part of Elohim and one without the other leaves us in an incomplete picture of Elohim. What would happen if we had continuous light and no darkness, it would mean our bodies which are designed to rest in darkness the time they replenish would not happen therefore this would leave us in an incomplete and weak state so darkness is very important for our bodily functions yet we imagine that darkness means evil which is only a human distinction but not necessarily an eternal one.

29

When I was a young boy I used to go walking through the graveyard to prove to myself that I am not afraid of the dark because it was simply a condition of a twenty-four hour cycle and nothing more. To be afraid of darkness is built into our psyche but in reality both darkness and light are part of the twenty-four hour day where no period is evil. While we come to understand in our worldview that Satan's ways must be dark meaning he is wicked so we have applied terminologies that we would like to understand. One could argue that these are only symbols while wickedness associated with darkness is only a cultural phenomenon and not a de-facto standard.

Hence why Iyob said:

> **Iyob 34:22** There is no darkness, nor shadow of death, where the workers of iniquity may hide themselves.

And king Dawud proclaimed:

> **Psalm 119:11** If I say, surely the darkness shall cover me; even the night shall be light about me.

Whether it is light or darkness these are but two binary distinctions and to YHWH it's the same as he can see in both and these are two sides of His being. In fact darkness is a handicap to us because we need lights to see but it's not a handicap to the creator of heaven and earth.

In the African culture black men would paint themselves white to reveal wicked spirits such as demons so in that culture the colour white was associated with evil and not black. The Bible is clear that Elohim can create evil and that He does create Evil while Christians usually misinterpret this for only natural disasters but indeed what El says He can do. He does bring evil upon nations in various forms.

> **Isaiah 45:7** I form the light, and create darkness: I make shalom (peace), and create evil: I YHWH do all these things.

Elohim creates evil e.g. not like humans where one plans to murder another (humans creates evil in the heart and act in the flesh) while Elohim's evil is usually to correct his people and not to do everlasting damage to someone. This may vary with such as a natural disaster or by sending a spirit to deceive a king as did happen in times past.

> **First Kings 22:22** And YHWH said to him, in what way? And he said, I will go forth, and I will be a lying ruach (spirit) in the mouth of all his prophets. And he said you shall persuade him, and prevail also: go forth, and do so.

Did YHWH send a lying spirit to deceive King Ahab or not? He indeed did, yet this may be construed as evil. YHWH created/made evil or allowed a situation to prevail but the end result was the betterment of His people who were being deceived by Ahab who was leading Israel astray into false elohim. One can see YHWH's purpose of evil is not the same as men who do it for personal gain but Elohim for the well of the whole of Israel.

If Elohim can create evil then what colour is evil can you tell? It's not black and not even white. Evil has whatever colour you decide to give it as it is without colour but one thing we do know that every culture around the world has given it its own colour and meaning. So the first thing we need to do when we want to learn the Bible is remove cultural issues and perceptions in which we grew up which will then leave us open to investigate and understand true biblical culture. To see the deeper spiritual significance of the Kingdom of Eloah we must open our mind to the culture of the Hebrew people who started their journey in Africa of all places.

Chapter 3
The Garden of Ayden

Who were the Israelites?

In order to answer this question we have to locate the Garden of Ayden so that we may understand where the first man was put which will then help us pinpoint true Israelites versus those who merely make false claims today.

> **Genesis 1:27** So Elohim <u>created</u> man in His own image(s), in the image(s) of Elohim He created him; <u>male</u> and <u>female</u> He created them.

We need to ask two questions here. Number one who was the first man (Adam) created after and number two who was the woman created after?

Elohim created the first man Adam (which in Hebrew means earth or mud) and the woman from the ground. Note both were created from the ground, earth mixed with water is black or very dark brown consistency and not white. The first woman was not called Chava (Eve) but her name has been obscured in the Bible because of her sin that she has been remembered no more but most people are oblivious to this fact because of church traditions and erroneous teachings which still circulate in churches today in which something is simply assumed to be true when it's not. Most people think the first woman was Chava but Chava was actually the <u>second</u> woman or what I term Adam's northern wife. Adam and his first wife (In the Southern region) were both created in Africa and I shall prove this point in a minute. They were both black as Africans are and they are our first ancestors. So if Rabbi Paulos who looked like an Egyptian (Egyptians were black) said the Messiah is the last Adam then what colour should be the last Adam since he resembles the first Adam, Pray tell?

> **Genesis 1:26** Then Elohim said, Let Us make humans in our image(s), according to our likeness...

Or we can put it another way if the first man was created after the image of Elohim there has to be a Template to make man and indeed there was a template that of the Messiah Yahushua which was used to fashion the first man. So if the first Adam is fashioned after the special body given to the Messiah in the heaven then what was the last Adam?

The first Adam and the last Adam have to have some resemblance which we will examine shortly.

Please note a body was indeed prepared for the Messiah as the book of Hebrews tells us from which we know that the first Adam was fashioned.

> **Psalm 40:6** Sacrifice and offering you did not desire; but a body you have prepared for me: burnt offering and transgression offering have you not required.

So if the body that was prepared for the Messiah looked like a black African with hair with locks then what would the first Adam look like? He would have to look identical in similar features because he was not only created in Africa but looked like an African. A man of that region. Elohim would not create a white man and put him in Africa because white skin would not last the heat of the sun for a few days and burn.

Messiah indeed has braided hair (locks) just like Africans. Caucasian/white people do not have braided hair or locks.

> **Revelations 1:14-15** His head and his **hairs were white like wool**, as white as snow; and his eyes were as a flame of fire; **15** And his feet like_fine brass, as if they burned in a furnace; and his voice as the sound of many waters.

The Messiah had woolly hair as black African men do and his feet like brass this is the colour of bronze or how African men look. The description is of someone standing in the sun.

Now coming back to the first woman and we will investigate her name which has been given in the Bible but as I said she has been obscured due to her sin based on the orders of Elohim.

The principle is in the Torah that those whose sins are judged and those who are guilty to be thrown into the lake of fire are blotted out of the book of life.

Exodus 32:33 And YHWH said to Musa (Moses), whoever has sinned against Me, I will blot him out of my scroll.

So what is the blotting out and how does it apply to a person male or female?

This means removing him or her from the book of life so that they may be remembered no more hence when Lilith the first woman was judged she was blotted out of the book of life forever. This is also why we do not see her name visibly mentioned in the bible but alluded to clearly in many other passages of Scripture.

Iyob 24:20 The womb shall forget him; the worm shall feed sweetly on him; he (Or She) shall be no more remembered; and wickedness shall be broken as an etz (tree).

This is the eternal law of YHWH our Elohim who does this for good measure. Wicked people are not remembered while the right-ruling are never forgotten this is the reason why the Yahudim celebrate the life of the dead and likewise we celebrate the death and resurrection of our Messiah.

Isaiah 34:14 The **wild beasts of the desert** shall also meet with the wild beasts of the island, and the wild goats shall cry to his fellow; **the night creature (Lilith)** also shall toss violently there, and find for herself a place for home.

The wild beasts of the desert in this verse are a reference to the demons alongside Lilith that live in dry places such as a desert. This entire chapter is about Arabia.

So what happened to Lilith? Lilith was created from the ground the same ground Adam was created from because the text says "**Elohim made them male and female**. " The woman was created or fashioned after the Holy Spirit who being feminine had the female qualities that were put into the woman. Lilith after creation started to fight with her husband Adam daily and not listen to him and wanted to be a co-equal in leadership. They were quarrelling all the time and there was no end in sight. She was disobedient to her husband Adam and then one day Lilith ran away with a rebellious angel to the land of Saudi Arabia and hid there in a cave where she married the angel. Since she went into adultery this greatly grieved Adam who knew not what to do, he tried to talk to her but she would not listen so Adam asked YHWH for help. She did not pay any attention to what he had to say. Sound familiar? This is the picture of many disobedient women today especially in the West where there freedom means they also have to rule over men.

Elohim then sent three angels which are mentioned in the *Alphabetum Siracidis* (*Sepher Ben Sira*) to ask her to repent and return but she would not. She was then turned into a demoness and she rebelled further by producing 100 demon children daily that she beget with the rebellious angel. Elohim then started to kill her offspring for her disobedience and held out the judgment for Lilith for the Day of Judgment but Lilith swore to retaliate upon man by killing his offspring. *Sefer Rasiel also mentioned the formula to make amulets with the angelic names.*

YHWH enactment of the Mazuza commandment which at heart is to protect the offspring of man to affix on the doorposts with YHWH's name in it the sacred name that guards and protects us from demonic spirits. The Rabbis advise their followers to hang Psalm 121 around beds and newly weds rooms to protect the marriage and would put amulets on the new born child's bedroom and cot by writing the name of the three angels to protect the new born child. This is both true and the right thing to do.

The three angels that were sent after Lilith were Senoi, Sansenoi, and Semangeloph and it is still a Jewish rabbinic custom to put amulets of these names upon newly born infants to protect them from Lilith's demonic children from killing the infant. In order to protect us from any demonic sprit we are to put YHWH the sacred name of our Elohim upon and around our places of abode, this is essential. Hence the commandment to put the Mazuza is part of this, which many still do not understand as it contains the most sacred name.

Genesis 2:20-23 And Ahdahm gave names to all cattle, and to the fowl of the air, and to every beast of the field; but for Ahdahm there was not found any helper[5] for him. **21** And YHWH Elohim caused a deep sleep to fall upon Ahdahm, and he slept: and he took Akhat[6] of his side bones,[7] and closed up the flesh there;[8]

The Creation of Ahdahm's Second/Third wives Chava, Ishah, the Beautiful Black women

22 And the side with the bone, which YHWH Elohim had taken from man, <u>he made woman</u>, and brought to the man.[9]

23 And Ahdahm said, at this reoccurrence, These standing in front of my face are bones of my bones, and flesh of my flesh: they shall be called Ishah (woman), because these were taken out of her Husband.

We are told by the writer of Genesis that there was no helper for Adam in the animal kingdom then YHWH put Adam to sleep to create the second/third woman. Remember YHWH forbids incest so Adam's children intermarried between the second ad third wife.

While all this went on in Africa then YHWH looked at Adam as he was very lonely and he decided that it was time for Adam to have his second wife who became known as Chava (life) popularly known as Eve though that is actually the name of a Babylonian false deity.

---

[5] Man was not designed to have a companion from the animal world but today most people are happy with their dogs but dogs and cats do not make helpers. In order to have a helper one must seek out a male or female according to petition to YHWH that would be suitable for a person.

[6] Plural ending word for one is "akhat" versus singular ending word "Akhad." See Gen 1:9 where it is singular Akhad while here it is plural Akhat with a Tav ending instead of a dalet.

[7] YHWH took Adam's SIDE, including his flesh, which can mean more than one rib. The same word is used in building the tent; Shemoth (Exodus) 26:20. One side of the tent consisted of twenty pieces of wood, therefore, we can not say with certainty, that it was a single rib. This is assumed by many; but is simply presumptuous.

[8] Please see footnote Exodus 26:26.

[9] More than one woman brought one at a time.

This time Chava was taken from Adam's side so that there would not be an issue of superiority and rulership and Elohim made sure that they both knew who the head was and what Chava's role in the marriage was.

Note one important fact that Chava was created in the North-East African region known as Israel and this is where we start to see the North/South axis that many African ruler/priests followed later even Abraham had African ancestors and his colour was black. The idea that the Bible figures were white started after the 15th century when Pope Julius II ordered all the paintings of the Messiah, Mary and others which showed him as black to be repainted as white after Michel Angelo's depiction of them as white Europeans. Before this event took place all the paintings of Madonna and the child (Miriam and her Son) were black and they looked as Africans.

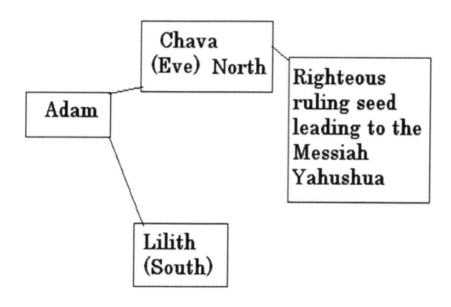

Fig1

The points to note with the first man and first woman were that they were created from the earth from the African soil and the first woman Lilith rebelled. She was turned into a demoness and her children who were demons are to this day trying to usurp the authority given to man and to throw down man through their leader Satan so they can rule and reign. So the battle in the spiritual realm is of rulership also.

The second woman was created from Adam and she was very faithful to Adam. What is important about this North/South axis? It was a common custom for people of African/Asian culture to place two wives who were in ruling clans one in the North and one in the South. The wife in the North usually was a niece or patrilineal cousin while the southern wife was a cousin bride of matrilineal descent. The reasons to marry in the family were to do with protecting the inheritance because it would remain in the same clan and family and not go to another clan.

These kinds of marriages are still very common in the east and can still be found practiced by some African tribes. Abraham had one wife from his father Terach's side with Sarah being his patrilineal relative (half sister) and the other with his mother's side his cousin bride Keturah in the south, while Sarah was in the North. One of Keturah's great grandfathers was Joktan so we know that Keturah's mother was the granddaughter of Joktan which was the wife of Terach. We look at the pattern of Keturah's children to arrive at this conclusion.

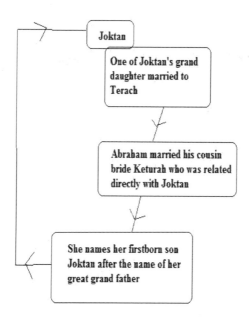

Fig2

Gen 10:26 – Joktan is mentioned in the Genealogy.
Gen 25:2 – Joktan is mentioned in the sons of Abraham. Note Jokshan and Joktan are identical names.

We can see that Terach Abraham's father also followed the same pattern. See diagram below.

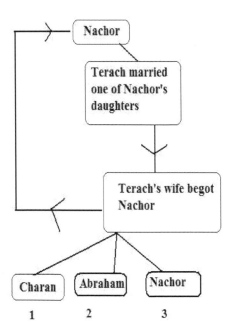

Fig3

Although the Genealogy lists Abraham first, Nachor and Charan next in Genesis 11:26 which makes it appear that Abraham is older but the eldest is actually Charan who was the ruling priest mentioned last.

Many usually assume that the first name in the list must be sequential and be the eldest but this is not always true. The Torah does not necessarily list names in order of age. These people such as Terach, Nachor were from the Horoite cultures hence why we see the hur in their names. Hur was also a sacred mountain for these people in Arabia which would then be classed as East-Africa all part of this one continent. This mountain is mentioned in Numbers 20:22. Don't get confused with the spelling of Hor or Hur they are interchangeable, however note many times geographers do not get their geography right by saying a place is in Egypt while it was in fact in South Arabia. The classic example is of the mountain of Sinai which is not in Egypt but Arabia.

The Horoites were the first people who believed that Horus was the Son of Elohim the son of Isis and that he was the wearer of the two crowns in the Egyptian religion and in the religion of the Nile delta. He was depicted as a man though believed to be divine. So one could say that Christianity did have at its heart a belief that started thousands of years ago by these people which predates the Christian teaching, even predating Judaism because the Horoites believed Horus to be the son of Elohim. We know the Messiah is the Son of Elohim so there was an expectation in Abraham's people to receive the personage of the Son of Elohim.

The placing of wives North and South was an interesting part of this pattern. In Kabbalah Jewish mystical studies of the Torah the North is the point for the numeric one which is related to Elohim and with heaven the abode of Elohim. The south is the point or numeral six on the face of a clock which is related to inheritance, rulership and descendants. Hence one can see why the two wives were placed opposite. The Egyptians circumcised their children both males and females were not allowed to stand in the presence of a king if they were not circumcised. Else they were considered unclean people. According to the African tradition they also circumcised their daughters long before Islam came to them. Note Egypt was fully part of Africa and so was Israel. Also note the use of meats we find the African pig consumption is the lowest considering since majority of these were Israelites they stuck to meats which were considered kosher such as goat, sheep, lamb and beef.

Also note female circumcision today is considered an act of mutilation by many but in the older days it was not seen in such a way and ancient people would laugh at today's so called experts but this act was seen to enhance the female characteristic of purity, virility and enhance fertility. Homosexuality exists more in European culture and Arab culture than any other culture. In African culture such things were not common because of the standard that was ascribed to men to be strong supporters of households and while the women were ascribed the other qualities. While homosexuality is nothing more than a weakness of men and perversion of the male role which was not acceptable to the African races and society therefore was shunned.

Abraham's father who also had two wives in the North from Nachor's daughters who when giving birth to her children calls her firstborn son's name Nachor. We find the three names in this genealogy revealed to us a tribal affinity such as the names Abram, Nachor and Charan or tribal chiefs.

Abraham was the youngest but not immediately the ruling prince of Terach's household and it was after Charan's death that he was the next in line to become the ruling prince. So one of Terach's wives was Nachor's daughters while his other wife was living in Beersheba the daughters from Joktan's clan.

The ruling prince usually was from the Northern wife in the case of Abraham it was Isaac and in the case of Adam it would be the Messiah the future prince. The North/South axis allowed priests to control two families and to control properties in both areas of the region also to protect resources such as land and water.

Abraham's people were people who controlled commodities such as water wells. The water was needed for the livelihood of people because without water you could not survive. We find in the Bible Abraham, Isaac and Jacob all controlled wells and were very rich men living near wells. Often disputes arose because of water as we find Isaac running into many disputes (Gen 26:20).

So to sum up the Garden of Ayden was in West Central Africa and ran towards East Africa. When Lilith ran away she ran away east to South Saudi Arabia to the cave which was also in the Mountain of YHWH. Her reasoning would be that she would be safe there but it was not to be.

Genesis 2:8 And YHWH Elohim planted a garden eastward in Ayden, and there he put the man whom he had formed.

When Lilith ran away there was no Garden planted at that time because that took place afterwards. Adam was then put into a Garden with boundaries and gates; the Garden was very large running from West Africa towards the East into several hundred miles. The second woman Chava was created for Adam from his side ribs (Note not a single rib) in the Garden. She was created in the North/East boundary of the Garden which extended into Israel. Her creation was likely in the area of central Eastern Jerusalem near Mount Maryah.

> **Genesis 2:15** And YHWH Elohim took the man, and put him into the garden of Ayden to work it and to guard it carefully.

We are told in Genesis 2:8 the Garden was planted and Adam was put there so where did YHWH take him from to put him in the Garden? He was outside first in the open land and was put inside this Garden which was full of vegetation to both protect him and

---

[10] http://maps.google.co.uk/maps?hl=en&tab=wl

assign him his duties as a test for him. The only place on earth that still holds similar greenery is Africa and no other lands hold similar vegetation. However the African landscape has changed after the fall but it was extremely luscious region at one time and there was no desert there at that time. These deserts are a change of landscape much later and as a result of punishment on Elohim's chosen.

In Genesis 1:27 the first woman had already been created and had left Adam. The purpose of the Garden was to protect Adam from the rebellious angels that had descended and wreaked havoc. There were at least three falls of the rebellious angels that we can identify from scripture. The first fall when Lilith was enticed and removed (Gen 1:27, Gen 3:1). The second fall when the Angels made a covenant to go and corrupt the women on the earth mentioned in Gen 6:2. There was a third fall which was much bigger revealed in the book of Revelation 12:7.

We are told in the Book of Enoch that the rebellion was caused by the Angels who objected to the creation of Adam.

> **Enoch Chapter 31:1-5** Ahdahm has life on eretz, and I created a garden in Ayden in the east, that he should observe the covenant and keep the command. **2** I made the shamayim open to him, that he should see the heavenly messengers singing the song of victory, and the gloomless light. **3** And he was continuously in paradise, and the devil understood that I wanted to create another world, because Ahdahm was Master on eretz, to rule and control it. **4** The devil is the evil ruach of the lower places, as a fugitive he made Sotona from the shamayim as his name was Satanail HaStan, thus he became different from the heavenly messengers, but his nature did not change his intelligence as far as his understanding of right-ruling and sinful things. **5** And he understood his condemnation and the sin which he had sinned before, therefore he conceived thought against Ahdahm, in such form he entered and seduced Chava, but did not touch Ahdahm.

Several things come to light. One Adam was not present when Chava was seduced he was somewhere else. The Rabbis think he may have been sleeping however he was not around at the discussion that took place with Chava and the serpent. Note the Garden was protected from angels that were planning to corrupt man.

Why was Satan so jealous of Adam? It appears from the text of Ezekiel 28:13 that Satan was put in the Garden to sing the praises of Elohim. He may also have been created there in that region as there is a hint in the passage of this declaring that he was adorned there with at least nine of the twelve precious stones of the High Priest. However pride got the better of him and he became extremely jealous of Adam, which caused him to entice a serpent and use him to deceive Chava so they were working in partnership and in the end all those that align with Satan will be punished.

This is why when Elohim punished Satan he also punished the serpent who originally could walk but later could only move upon his belly. One has to ask why would Elohim punish the poor snake if it was Satan doing the bidding, the reason is that he entered into the scheme of Satan and the serpent was looking for self glory which did not come to pass. Note in the passage when Chava is talking

> **Genesis 3:2** And the woman said unto the serpent, we may eat of the fruit of the etzim (trees) of the garden:

People automatically assume that this was Satan but the text does not say this. If the text was going to say it was Satan then it would have used the terms of reference to indicate this. The snake's agenda according to Rabbi David Fohrman and the Midrashim[11] was that Adam will eat the fruit and he will die then the snake can marry Chava to rule and reign to reclaim her for the animal kingdom. This is why he was deceiving her because the serpent was jealous that Elohim had made a separate creation for Adam while he was part of the common creation. However this makes no sense because the snake could not have human children so the marriage agenda does not really add up. The Hebrew word used for "cunning" is the same word used for 'naked', however here the term 'naked' means he came with a deceiving agenda to dethrone man from his position.

---

[11] http://www.aish.com/jl/b/eb/ge/48962006.html

The text also shows us a pact between Satan and the serpent so that Satan can rule and reign and the serpent will be his number two in charge so to speak but first they must remove Adam and then the serpent had gone forward to do the evil deed for Satan.

Some Christian groups have run away with the idea of something called serpent seed meaning that the snake had sexual relations with Chava and therefore Cain was born. Such groups lack Torah knowledge because this did not happen. The text is clear in Lev 18:23-29 that any such soul would be removed and had Chava being involved in such an act of sin she would be killed by Elohim and that would be the end of the present human race as we know it. Maybe then Elohim would have to create a third woman but we know that did not happen.

Satan had looked at a coup in which he will use the serpent to dethrone the man so the serpent gets the blame while he pretends to be innocent party of the crime and then in a double twist he will over throw Elohim but he was doomed to failure. This also reveals Satan has limited capacity to think and understand the nature of Elohim. The word used for "naked" in Genesis 2:25 is Arum for naked and it is the same word used for the snake and his cunning. The term naked in Genesis 2:25 does not mean without clothes but without agendas. They were covered by a special light.

The text in Genesis 3:1 used the word Arum for the word "cunning" for the serpent, this word could equally show us the three letter root Resh, Vav and Mem (רום) for rum "to be exalted." The serpent had an agenda with Satan to exalt himself but failed. The spelling of the two words is the same except that the preceding Hebrew letter ayin ע shows us the picture of the haughty eyes in which the serpent had his eyes set on exalting self. They were trying to remove the man from his rightful place. While Chava ate the fruit and took the fruit and later went to her husband and gave it to him to eat. Adam's fault was not enquiring how the woman came in possession of the fruit and eating it.

> **Ezekiel 28:14-15** You are the anointed cherub that covers; and I have set you so: **you were upon the Set-Apart mountain of Elohim**; you have walked up and down in the

midst of the stones of fire. **15** You were perfect in your ways from the day that you were created, till iniquity was found in you.

Satan had been at the place which was the Mountain of Elohim in Saudi Arabia but his pride got in the way of things as even it does with many men and hence his fall.

Isaiah 14:13 For you have said in your heart, <u>I will ascend into the shamayim (heavens),</u> I will exalt my throne above the stars of El: I will **sit also upon the Mount of the congregation**, in the sides of the north:

What the prophet tells us here is indeed quite deep that Satan had said he will ascend into the shamayim. To ascend is to understand that he wanted to receive honour and worship just as YHWH does.

And here the plural for <u>heavens</u> tells us Satan wanted to ascend to the ten heavens and sit on YHWH's throne and be exalted. How a created being could think that it's hard to imagine but we know many humans have also tried to replace YHWH by declaring themselves as Elohim but their end result is death. Note the text says "I will exalt my throne above the stars of El". The Hebrew is e-ele mi-mael lecho-chavi El arim.

This raises the question why would an angel have a throne since he was the leader for the worship choir and no ordinary one at that? This reveals that though initially Satan worshipped Elohim but he became very prideful where he wanted to be worshipped in the same way and others would sing his glories instead of Elohim's which would have led to his throne being made, this was first created in his thought process followed by the actual throne which we know now rests spiritually in Turkey (Rev 2:12-13).

Who were the Israelites?
Now that we know the location of the Garden then it makes it easier for us to answer our question. The Israelites were black Hebrew people very African looking indeed. When we look at the practices that are mentioned in the Bible one cannot ignore this unless he is totally ignorant of African practices and biblical culture. One thing believers forget is that Israel is still a part of

Africa in fact North-East Africa because the term middle-east is a fairly new term which was invented in the 19th century by the British. There was no such term in 2000 CE calling the place or landmass of Israel the middle-east.

> **Hos 11:10** (KJV) They shall walk after the LORD: he shall roar like a lion: when he shall roar, then the children shall **tremble from the west**.

The term west here does not refer to western lands but to West Africa which is West of Israel. The term is more accurately used in the AF Bible as Tremble from the Sea.

> **Hosea 11:10** (HTHS) They shall walk after YHWH: he shall roar like a lion: when he shall roar, then the sons shall come **trembling from the sea**.

12

As you can see in the map above that the whole continent of Africa lies West of Israel then we find Brazil and North America also left of Israel which is its West. This indicates to us that many Israelites would have ended up in these nations and we know the slave trade caused many black people to end up in Europe and America. A point of note about African culture that today you see this fashion both in the European countries and America of people

---

[12] http://maps.google.co.uk/

getting their bodies pierced from everywhere of the bellybutton to the eyes, ears, tongue and private parts also../Piercing the body was very common in ancient African culture and hence why it was forbidden in the Torah. This indicates to us that there is a little African coming out of many people in the west because they contain the blood of Africans whether they believe it or not.

On December 21st 2010 there was a lunar eclipse, in the ancient times the lunar and solar eclipses were watched by people but in the In the African culture the lunar eclipse does not hold much significance as much as the solar eclipse. Since the moon merely reflects the light of the sun it is the sun that is believed to reflect the light of Elohim in an allegorical way. This is why many religions in the world were sun centred and not moon centred. The people who fell into worship of the moon or the elohim sin were the people of Turkey, Iraq and Arab lands. This El later came to be known as Allah which the Muslims worship.

The el had three daughters though some contest maybe two daughters and one consort. The Bible speaks about such phenomenon calling the Messiah the Sun of Righteousness (Mal 4:2). Egyptian monarchs though themselves African and black painted their wives with white faces as can be seen in some Egyptian mummies. These women were not white in complexion but only in ascribing attributes of the moon being white and reflecting the light of the sun. The female characteristics were taken from the moon hence the planet Venus. Her monthly cycle was considered to be regulated by the cycles of the moon.

So the restoration is from the Western African lands and generally of African people first and not white Caucasians or of Mulattoes (Mixed white) people. What does a mulatto look like? Look at Moroccans today who are of white colour they are the classical mulattoes. That is how they would look and resemble very similar to the white Caucasians. So it's black first then followed by the mixture of white.

One question often arises for China what will happen to them. While many people may not know that the common ancestor of the Chinese people was also a black African. The original Buddha was black. Here is evidence from an excavation in 1972 near

Anyang which you can see on the next page with pictures to see what it reveals.

> [13]The analysis suggested that modern Africans are descended from 14 ancestral populations, which generally correlate with known language and cultural groups. But most African populations show high levels of mixed ancestry, reflecting historic migrations across the continent – such as the movement of Bantu speakers from the highlands of Nigeria and Cameroon across much of eastern and southern Africa in the past 5000 years.
>
> The researchers had expected to find a close relationship between language and genetics. "The spread of a language into a new area normally involves the spread of at least some speakers," says Christopher Ehret, a specialist in African history and linguistics at the University of California, Los Angeles, and a member of Tishkoff's team. "Gene flow is simply the normal accompaniment."
>
> But migrations can also cause genes and language to diverge. For example, the researchers found that pygmy populations from central Africa cluster genetically with eastern and southern African speakers of languages that rely heavily on clicking of the tongue. Despite retaining their distinct genetic heritage, pygmies seem to have lost their ancestral languages as Bantu speakers moved in.
>
> The results suggest that all modern humans can trace their origin to a population that lived near the border between South Africa and Namibia – although Tishkoff stresses that these people may have moved into the area from elsewhere. As expected, the study also places the exit point for humanity's great "out of Africa" migration near to the Red Sea.

Note the RED SEA as I have suggested the common ancestors of humanity Adam and Chava.

---

[13] http://www.newscientist.com/article/dn17057-huge-gene-study-shines-new-light-on-african-history.html

50

Here is what a historian had to say on this:

> According to the imminent scholar and sage Runoko
> Rashidi the Chinese have come from African ancestors.
>
> [14]"Funan is the name given by Chinese historians to the
> earliest kingdom of Southeast Asia. Its builders were a
> Black people known as <u>Khmers</u>, a name that loudly recalls
> ancient Kmt (Egypt).In remote antiquity the Khmers seem
> to have established themselves throughout a vast area that
> encompassed Myanmar, Kampuchea, Laos, Malaysia,
> Thailand and Vietnam..."
>
> "Although many are startled by the notion, it is absolutely
> undeniable, that: as the first hominids and modern humans;
> as simple hunter-gatherers and primitive agriculturists; as
> heroic warriors and premier civilizers; as sages and priests,
> poets and prophets, kings and queens; as deities and
> demons of misty legends and shadowy myths; and yes,
> even as servants and slaves, the Black race has known
> Asia intimately from the very beginning. Even today, after
> an entire series of holocausts and calamities, the numbers
> of Blacks in Asia approach two-hundred million."

---

[14] http://www.essaysbyekowa.com/Black%20Buddha.htm

Chariots of the Black Shang of China - 1800 to 1100 BC

I. Er-li-tuo (2,200 - 1800 BC)

II. Shang

III. Shang Chariot burial with driver and two horses

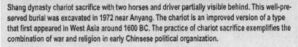

Shang dynasty chariot sacrifice with two horses and driver partially visible behind. This well-preserved burial was excavated in 1972 near Anyang. The chariot is an improved version of a type that first appeared in West Asia around 1600 BC. The practice of chariot sacrifice exemplifies the combination of war and religion in early Chinese political organization.

LEGEND: When the question of the early appearance of the chariot in China is brought up, never is it realized what these images show - that the earliest Chinese and the ones who brought civilization to China were, by phenotype, Africans. This is evident with the Er-li-tuo of the upper picture and the Shang images, shown in the column. Neither is it known or acknowledged that the so-called "Asian" chariot of which the Shang is a type, was used in the Altaic mountains of Siberia by, the phenotypic remains of the people show, Africans who were equestrians.

15

---

[15] http://www.beforebc.de/Related.Subjects/The.Equestrian.Age/51-06-02.html

16   Chinese Laughing Buddah

This is a very late depiction of Buddah with the fat stomach however ancient Buddha was not only black but referred to priests who were considered the enlightened ones.

Here are some images of the ancient Buddha of India

Note the Negroid African features.

[16] http://www.africaresource.com/rasta/articles/african-roots-of-china-a-picture-is-worth-a-thousand-words/

We taught the system to every nation. Godfrey Higgins the writer of Anacalpysis wrote:

> "The <u>originals of all the Gods</u> have always been of the black race." The ancients viewed the sacred image of the Divine as Black. And *woolly* hair was a sign of divinity - called "the hair of the gods."

Olmecs of America

[17]'In my Essay on *The Celtic Druids*, I have shown, that a great nation called Celtæ, of whom the Druids were the priests, spread themselves almost over the whole earth, and are to be traced in their rude gigantic monuments from India to the extremities of Britain. Who these can have been but the early individuals of the *black* nation of whom we have been treating I know not, and in this opinion I am not singular.'

The Buddha was a caste of Priests that brought particular Gospel to the Middle East, India and Asia. Their root was in Africa 'the land of the Blacks'. When you look to culture and religion Science and Technology everything without exception is African born.

Gerald Massey and the goddesses:

"The genetrix represented as Dea Multimammia - the Diana of Ephesus, is found as a black figure, nor is the hue mystical ONLY, for the features are Negroid as were those of the black Isis in Egypt."

---

[17] http://www.essaysbyekowa.com/Black%20Buddha.htm

Isis

What does this mean? All the Goddesses, including Mary were African in origin brought to all continents by way of an African Priesthood. The Five precepts are:

> I undertake the precept to refrain from harming living creatures (killing).
> I undertake the precept to refrain from taking that which is not freely given (stealing).
> I undertake the precept to refrain from sexual misconduct. [Fornication and Adultery.]
> I undertake the precept to refrain from incorrect speech (lying, harsh language, slander, idle chit-chat).
> I undertake the precept to refrain from intoxicants which lead to loss of mindfulness. [Drunkenness, drug abuse]

Anyone can see that these sound and read a lot like the precepts from the Bible and that is essentially what they were. Buddha in fact enlightened priests were met by Yahushua when he went to India as a child and gave them his wisdom. He grew up with Yosef of Arimathaea who adopted him (See the book by Rabbi Simon Beyth Yahushua, the Son of Tzadok, The son of Dawud) and took him to journeys to India.

According to Gerald Massey:

[18]'It is **certain** that the Black Buddha of India was imaged in the 'Negro' type. In the **Negro Elohim**, whether called Buddha or Sut-Nahsi [Nehesi] we have datum. They carry their color in the proof of their origin. The people who first fashioned and worshipped the divine image in the Negroid mold of humanity must, according to ALL knowledge of human nature, have been Negroes themselves. <u>For blackness is not merely mystical, the features and hair of Buddha belonged to the Black Race</u> and Nahsi [Nehesi] is the Negro name. Volume 1pp.18, 218 - A Book of Beginnings.

---

[18] http://www.essaysbyekowa.com/Black%20Buddha.htm

Africoid: her entire faceless head is covered with woolly hair like that of Buddha's.

Venus of Willendorf

Buddha, 12th century (sitting), 9th century (top inset), and 11th century (bottom inset).

The text in the picture says 12th century Buddha.

Mr. Wilsford, in his treatise on Egypt and the Nile, in the Asiatic Researches, informs us, that many very ancient statues of the Elohim Buddha in India have crisp, curly hair, with flat noses and thick lips; and adds,

"Nor can it be reasonably doubted, that a race of Negroes formerly had power and pre-eminence in India."

"And the learned Mathematician, Reuben Burrow, has no hesitation in pronouncing Stonehenge to be a temple of the black, curly-headed Buddha. [Anacalpysis, Godfrey Higgins - 1833]."

Hoshea 11:11 They shall <u>**tremble as a bird out of Mitzrayim**</u> (Egypt), and as a <u>**dove out of the land of Assyria**</u>: and I will place them in their houses, says YHWH.

Now when we look at Hoshea with a clear mind we can see what is it that he is trying to tell us. Hoshea 11:10 tells us that they will come from the West (Sea), therefore West would be the specific location of Israel's westerly direction and that starts with Africa immediately. So where should our focus be for restoration? In Africa of course and if we are not working in Africa then we will be breaking the focal point of the largest Hebrew Israelites. The above text in Hoshea 11:11 tells us what immediate lands the restoration involves. Well Mitzrayim which means burnt face or black face is the modern country of Egypt which is in North Africa and the text also describes Assyria which are the lands surrounding Egypt such as Syria, Iran, Iraq, South Eastern Turkey and even parts of Arabia.

If we examine one such example in the Bible we can see that many obscured texts actually help us to trace people and their ancestors.

First Samuel 2:3 And Dawud sent and enquired after the

woman. And one said, Is not this Batsheba (Bathsheba), the daughter of Eliyam, the wife of **Uri'yah the Hittite**?

We find here one of the wives of King David who was first the wife of Uriyah who died in battle due to King David who was enamoured with Bathsheba and wanted to marry her. Note Hitties were black people and Bathsheba was also a black woman, King David himself was black and I will explain that in a minute.

Let us examine Bathsheba first. In the days of Israel's rule and reign when people were given names they were meant to be a reference to the person in some way so the name was related to a person in certain ways. For instance when King Solomon was born he was given this name which has the word Shalom in it meaning peace so the Hebrew name for King Shlomo is a variant of peace meaning the same thing. This king also had the most peaceful reign of the majority of the kings of Israel. One of his sons was taken into Ethiopia by the Queen of Sheba whose son had descendants reigning in Ethiopia until the 20th century. You can check a name called Menelek II, he was a descendant of King Solomon, and he was not only a great ruler but the only one who defeated the Italians in a humiliating defeat in Ethiopia. Now Bathsheba in Hebrew means the daughter of Sheba and we can trace her father from her name.

> **Beresheeth (Gen) 10:7** The sons of Cush were; Sheba, Chavilah, Sabtah, Raamah, and Sabtechah; and the sons of Raamah were Sheba and Dedan.

Note that Sheba was the son of Cush and that is the line for Bathsheba. So King David was married to a grand daughter of Cush and Cush as we all know was black one of the descendants of the African people.

Now coming to King David that he was black but many automatically assume that he was white by misreading certain texts.

> **First Sam 17:42** (KJV) And when the Philistine looked about, and saw David, he disdained him: for he was *but* a youth, and ruddy, and of a fair countenance.

Many reading the above text assume two things that King David was white and ruddy means red so only white have red or rosy complexion. If this is what you think then both of the above assumptions are false and misreading of the text.

Here is an accurate translation from the HTHS Bible.

> **First Samuel 17:42** And when the Philistine looked about, and saw Dawud, he disdained him: for he was but a youth, and of mahogany look, and of a fair countenance.

King David was ruddy which means of mahogany complexion and his son (King Solomon) he produced with Bathsheba was jet black. The Hebrew word for red that is used in the Bible is Admonee (Strong's H132) while it correctly means mahogany coloured and not just red. People automatically assume this means white however it does not. The Hebrew word used for white in the Torah is Laban which was also the brother of Rebecca while noting that he was an African and albino and two the same word is used for the word in leprosy for white spots on the skin as a sign of the disease and we find no such usage in the description of King David.

> **Leviticus 13:4** If the bright spot be white (Laban) in the skin of his flesh.

This tells us the colour of judgment in scripture was white. We also note that in African culture they would often paint their faces with white paint to depict evil spirits. This helps us to see who is who in the Bible.

Moses was a black man of North African descent and when he delivered the daughters of Reu'el they said the following:

> **Shemoth (Exo) 2:19** And they said, **A Mitzri (Egyptian)** delivered us from the hand of the shepherds, and he also drew enough mayim (water) for us, and watered the flock.

They said **an Egyptian** saved us? Did Moses show his passport and nationality or was it from his appearance that the girls concluded that he was an Egyptian (Black face)?

Did Zipporah conduct an interview of Moses? No. So we can conclude based on the evidence supplied that people knew **the skin colour of the Egyptians was dark**. Now ask yourself what colour were the ancient Egyptians? As a South-Easterner I can tell you instantly when I see a South-Indian or North-Indian because I can recognize them from the shading of the skin colour and I can even tell you when I see a Sri Lankan so likewise Zipporah was not incorrect in her assumption to place him from Egypt though He was Hebrew of course.

Now let us start to unfold what I am talking about. Why do we need to look at the African model? We are told in Scripture that Abraham's children and ancestors controlled major waterways. Isaac dug wells and controlled the water (Gen 26:15) Jacob his son likewise dug wells and controlled the water.

Anyone who controlled the water would be like a king in terms of wealth. We even find Reuel Moses's father in law near a water well controlling water (Exodus 2:16). Moses's second wife Zipporah was a Midianite woman from the line of Media who was a son of Joktan the ancestor of the pure Arabs and they were black. Joktan was Eber's son (Gen 10:25) from where the Hebrews have come so two lines run to the Hebrews if you follow the line of Abraham but no one will ever teach you this because of prejudice against the Arabs.

This then brings us closer to why scripture calls the sons of Tsiyon blacker than a coal.

Now we can certainly understand the following statement about the sons of Tsiyon...

> **Lam 4:2** The precious sons of Tsiyon, comparable to fine gold ...

> **Lam 4:8** Their visage is **blacker than a coal**...

Whether coal is healthy or sick it will always be black. This brings us to the conclusion that one the large majority of the Hebrew people were black and still are also, that the most sincere to obey and follow Torah would be black people today this is a sure fact. The largest Torah following congregation in the world today is in Nigeria which ranks a million members. Though they may not be entirely accurate how they obey and follow Torah but the desire is there never the less to serve Ha'Shem.

Some more pictures of what Hebrew Israelites looked like below.

19

Note the Hebrew slaves in Egypt and look at their head and skin colour. What do you see a Caucasian or Black Hebrew?

---

[19] http://sarabe3.tripod.com/israeliteimages.html

COPY OF WALL PAINTING IN TOMB OF IPUI AT THEBES,
13TH CENTURY B.C.; METROPOLITAN MUSEUM OF ART, NEW

A Hebrew water slave boy. Note his beard. This boy is assumed to be about 15 years of age. Notice his head has locked hair as blacks do.

Hebrews Israelites entering Egypt circa 1877 B.C.E. Note the women wearing different woollen coloured clothes. These are black perhaps brown coloured Hebrews.

Notice the Hebrew women all wearing different fancy clothes made of wool.

Notice the sons of Shem how they look. They all have beards and are wearing tzitzits on their clothes. Once again black Israelites.

Notice the sons of Japheth are Caucasian (white) and have tattoos on their skins. They do not have tizzies on their garments as the Hebrews.

Close up of Hebrew man and notice his woolly skirt and his Tzitzits made of wool in different colours of blue and red. He has a beard. Notice his hair is woolly as African men have it.

Notice the captive of Remesses II holding the locks of a Hebrew man.

Close up of the locks of hair. Unmistakable African looking

Prisoners of the Assyrians believed to be from around 680
BCE. Note the braided kinky hair.

Israelites led into the Assyrian Exile.

A close up of the Israelites. Look at their faces. They have not only kinky beards but braided (Locks). These are black Israelites. Caucasians do not have such hair.

A Close up of a Hebrew Musicians hair and beard. Look at the locks in the hair. Does this look like a white European or Black African?

One question that arises that if these black people are true Israelites then one can begin to understand why we would find them in Africa and why YHWH would restore them back from Africa. Admittedly there are many blacks who ended up through the slave trade into Europe and North America which are likely the Hebrew Israelites so when black people make this claim it can be taken seriously.

However what about the present people in Israel claiming to be Jews in Israel? It is well known fact amongst knowledgeable people that the present Ashkenazim Jews in Israel are not Semitic Hebrew Israelites but are European people. In fact in Israel you will be lucky if you find 20% of the population of true Hebrew Israelites. One such group that are true Semites are the Ethiopian Jews known as the flashas (Meaning black).

Another question that arises from the first is that if Elohim knew that the original Semites were not yet going back into the land then does He tell us anywhere that these are not the Semites. The answer to both the first question and the second question is answered by Elohim in the book of Genesis but is a little hidden. We will examine that prophecy but we will reference two different bibles to do that so you can see how it is hidden. Note the picture I showed you above for the sons of Japheth they are clearly white and it is they that are present in large numbers in Israel calling themselves Yahudim today.

> **Gen 9:27** (KJV) Elohim shall enlarge Japheth, and he shall dwell in the tents of Shem; and Canaan shall be his servant.

If someone was to look at this prophecy he will see nothing here of interest but simply a form of benediction that the sons of Japheth will go to see the Shemites (Real Yahudis) and be in collaboration with them in worship etc.

If you thought this then it's really time for enlightenment and to understand what Elohim has allowed to happen. The word that we are interested to look at is the word translated 'enlarge' which is used here in the text. Let me now show you this word in the AF Hebraic Study bible Second edition.

74

Beresheeth (Gen) 9:27 Elohim will allow Yapet to be deceived and he will dwell in the tents of Shem; and Canaan will become his servant.

The Hebrew word that is used here is the Hebrew term פתה (Patah) which does have one meaning to 'enlarge.' However its true meaning is not 'enlarge' in the context of this passage in Genesis 9:27. Now we will look at the true meaning.

Exodus 22:16 And if a man entices (Patah) a virgin who is not betrothed, and lies with her, he shall surely pay the bride-price for her to be his wife.

So what did the man do? It can be seen in two ways, one that he encouraged the girl to sleep with him and two he deceived the girl to deflower her in order to marry him so the term 'entice' here really means he "deceived" here. As the girl was deceived she slept with him prior to marriage and then she would no longer be a virgin. Perhaps for modern Western girls this is something to be proud of to sleep around before marriage and break their virginity but in the East it is a very shameful act and not only that it was but it still is very shameful because girls only break their virginity through their husband and not boyfriends as in the Western culture.

In the Eastern culture very few people would be willing to marry a girl who was not a virgin as it shows the purity of a girl before marriage. This kind of information is lost on western debased culture which is heavily into adultery and prostitution.

Deut 11:16 Take heed to yourselves, that your heart be not deceived (Patah), and you turn aside, and serve other Elohim, and worship them;

In Deuteronomy it is very clear that the word could not be used as 'enlarge' or 'encourage' but only deceive. If you are still not clear then the next passage will make it abundantly clear. These are the first three occurrences of the word and the fourth will make it clear what it should be.

Judges 14:15 And it came to pass on the seventh day that they said to Shimshon (Samson)'s wife, Entice

(Patah) your husband, that he may declare to us the riddle, lest we burn you and your father's house with fire: have you invited us to take what is ours? Is it not so?

So what did the Philistines do? They asked Samson's wife to deceive her husband and one can see absolutely clearly here that the word's primary meaning is to deceive. One cannot say that Samson's wife was 'encouraging' him because he would be taken prisoner and have his eyes removed. We then come back to answer the question in Genesis 9:27. Let us look at it again.

> **Beresheeth (Gen) 9:27** Elohim will allow Yapet to be deceived and he will dwell in the tents of Shem; and Canaan will become his servant.

Elohim will deceive Yapheth to dwell in the houses of Shem (The real Jews). So what happened was that the sons of Japheth were deceived into believing that they are the real Yahudis and so much so that today they claim the land of Israel as their own while they have no connection to the land of Israel but because of this both the sons of Japheth and Christians largely are deceived believing that the present occupiers of Israel are Jewish but they are really Edomites and the sons of Japheth.

The Rabbis see this prophecy as the sons of Javan going to fellowship with Shem in his Temple however this is not an accurate interpretation of this text. The words in Genesis 9:27 are unmistakable that he will dwell in the tents of Shem so where is Shem. Shem is of course not there. It does not say that both will dwell in the same house but that he will completely occupy the house of Shem. Today white Jews who claim to be Hebrews occupy the land mass that belongs to Shem but Shem who mixed with Ham in intermarriages has many descendants who are black and they are in very small numbers to be seen in Israel but ignorant Christians support the sons of Japheth to occupy the land that belongs to Shem.

> **Genesis 9:20** And Noakh began to be a farmer, and he planted a vineyard: **21** Then he drank of the wine, and was drunk; and became uncovered in his tent. **22** And Cham, the abbah of Canaan, saw the nakedness of his abbah, and told his two brothers outside. **23** But Shem and

Yapheth took a garment, laid it on both their shoulders, and went backward and covered the nakedness of their abbah: their faces were turned away, and they did not see their abbah's nakedness. **24** So Noakh awoke from his wine, and knew what his younger son had done to him. **25** Then he said, Cursed be Canaan; a servant of servants he shall be to his brethren. **26** And he said, Benevolent is YHWH, the Elohim of Shem; and may Canaan be his servant. **27** Elohim will entice Yapheth, and he will dwell in the tents of Shem; and may Canaan be his servant.

Something terrible happened yet to many readers of the bible they are clueless as to what really happened here to this day until they read this account that I will present from the AF Study Bible. How could a man so sober and so upright emerge from the destruction of many living things on the earth to just get drunk in his home and not know what is going on and yet this is what the text tells us.

The Ashkenazim Jewish rabbis come with elaborate theories reasoning that Noakh could not have done this on his own, maybe Ham poisoned him. One theory put forward by the Jewish rabbis which is totally erroneous is that Elohim Cursed Ham and turned him and his future sons black as a result of the curse because he tried to castrate Noakh while he was drunk.

The Babylonia Talmud a book dealing with ancient texts and the commentaries says the following to put down Ham and his sons according to rabbinic tradition.

> The Babylonian Talmud 108b –
> Go forth from the ark, thou, and thy wife, and thy sons, and thy sons' wives with thee. Whereon R. Johanan observed: From this we deduce that cohabitation had been forbidden. Our Rabbis taught: Three copulated in the ark, and they were all punished — the dog, the raven, and Ham. The dog was doomed to be tied; the raven expectorates [his seed into his mate's mouth]. and Ham was smitten in his skin. [Underscore mine]

From the above Talmudic quote circa 500 CE it was deduced that sexual cohabitation was forbidden on the ark but Ham did not restrict himself and the dog or the raven hence they were punished. Apparently Ham slept with his wife by a magical demon and Noakh caught him because of his footprints leading to his wife's bedroom. They believed that Ham had mocked Noakh's nakedness and invited his brothers to do the same so hence the wrath of Noakh on Ham.

Now let us look at actually what actually did happen thanks to a personal friend Rabbi Matthew Nolan, Oregon USA one of the faithful believers of the Messiah Yahushua. The following quotation is taken from the AF Netzarim Hebraic Study Bible thanks to Rabbi Matthew for the commentary.

> By Rabbi Matthew Nolan, Torah to the Tribes, Oregon, USA, 2009
> The Patriarchal family of Noakh.
>
> The question arises as to why Canaan was cursed by Noakh? Why not curse Ham himself, or Cush or Put or Mitzrayim? By unfolding our Beresheeth narrative a little further than the traditional story, one of Noakh getting drunk and Ham coming in and looking at his naked father, we will soon discover Noakh's patriarchal roots. My suggestion is that Noakh and Ham were enjoying the fruits of Noakh's vineyard, in Noakh's tent, when Noakh passed out.
>
> Ham then went into the adjoining chamber, and slept with Noakh's wife. He then came out being loose lipped because of his merriment, told his brothers. They then, backed into the tent and covered their father's wife; thereby covering their 'father's nakedness.' Canaan was the child of this union which is why Noakh cursed Canaan.
>
> The Canaanites were well known in the Torah, for their perverse sexual practices, which we are warned to avoid in Vayikra (Leviticus). A despicable trait of sexual immorality was passed down through the generational line birthed out of Ham's sin that took place in Noakh's tent (Beresheeth 9:22). What happened is the very thing that Rav Sha'ul disciplined the Corinthians for, a man slept with one of his father's wives (Qorintyah Alef 5:1). Yet in our narrative we

know that only one of Noakh's wives made it onto the ark. Sefer Ha Yashar, and Sefer Ha Yovel/Jubilees tell us of Noakh's wives.

One named Emzara, the daughter of Rakeel, who did not make it onto the ark (Jubilees 4:33). The other named Naamah, Noakh's wife, the daughter of Enoch, who was not Ham's mother, and who did make it onto the ark (Yashar 5:12). Our text in Vayikra/Leviticus 18:7 & 18:8 supports this by clarifying the phrase for Ham's sin as 'uncovering your father's nakedness', which means sleeping with your father's wife (Naamah) who is not your mother. The nakedness of your mother is 'her nakedness', but the term used in Beresheeth 'your father's nakedness', is in reference to the nakedness of your father's wife that was uncovered i.e. slept with.

It is also important to note that Abraham lived with Noakh for thirty nine years (Yashar 9:5) and learned the instructions of YHWH and His ways. This is clearly where Abraham learned to order his house into a patriarchal one, that was, kadosh/Set-Apart, and acceptable to YHWH, just like Noakh before him.

I believe the explanation is quite clear following the Torah guidelines that the Patriarchs were polygamous and it was or is not a sin to do so hence we still see these practices widely practiced in African and Muslim culture. Noakh had two wives and so did people before him and after him. The Bible clearly shows us a culture of North/South divide where ruling chiefs would place one wife in the North and one in the South. Abraham did this too. His wife Sarah was in the North (Hebron) and his wife Keturah was in the South (Bathsheba). We find the same pattern in Abraham's father Terach, see Fig 3 above.

However this is not to say that Ham became black as a result of the curse, unfortunately this is a product of wild imagination and legends. Ham was originally black skinned and so were Shem and Japheth. When I use the term black skinned I mean of any shade whether light brown, dark brown, black or dark black but they were not Caucasians but of African origins. This is evident from their previous forefathers such as Cain who travelled to Nod. Nod is linguistically equivalent to the Housa (African language) word for Nok.

This culture existed in the central Nigeria region where Cain initially went (Gen 4:16) and lived with his wife. He was a metal worker and builder. Even to this day metal workers in that region of the world keep two wives one North and one south. Nok is derived from the word Enoch. This is a title and not a name for the chief. Enoch was the ancestor of Abraham and he too was in the African regions. Enoch was African. Noakh's family being African had a strange thing happened to them at the birth of Noakh. This is what is described in the book of Enoch.

> **Enoch 105:10-12** And now, my father, hear me; for to my son Lamech a child has been born, who resembles not him; and whose nature is not like the nature of man. His colour is whiter than snow; he is redder than the rose; the hair of his head is whiter than white wool; his eyes are like the rays of the sun; and when he opened them he illuminated the whole house. **11** When also he was taken from the hand of the midwife, **12** His father Lamech feared, and fled to me, believing not that *the child* belonged to him

Noakh though an African was born an Albino completely white even his hair was white and his father was so afraid of this that he ran away. Noakh's hair was like white wool well only African children have woolly hair just as it was of Yahushua also who was black as will be revealed in this book later.

So the idea that Noakh cursed his son to be black is really irrational and nonsensical. Even in Islam black people were put down by suggesting that those in hell have black faces. Unfortunately these things were going to be used against the black people and they were going to be put down because they being Hebrew Israelites had transgressed the commandments of YHWH and YHWH was going to punish His people as He had said.

This is why even though the punishment is over the black people have suffered the greatest holocaust more than any other nation. Even white Jews do not compare to the suffering of the blacks to this day.

The modern Jews did suffer pogroms and the Holocaust largely due to identifying themselves with the Hebrews who as now you would know were originally black and many today still are.

However out of all this gloomy picture one good news comes that Yahushua came for His people the Hebrew Israelites to restore them back and has been restoring them back to Torah and covenants of Israel while much more work needs to be done but many blacks are now on the road to be restored first in mind, body and then later physically into the land of Israel at the appointed time.

Chapter 4
The Bible: A History of the Black Semitic people

Some people may find it odd to read the above title for this chapter. However if we are honest with ourselves and read the narratives in the Bible then we may realize that the Bible is indeed a history of a people that were settled in Africa. Israel not only was but still is in Africa what is today described as the Middle-East was first referred to as North-Eastern Africa.

It is evident to any sensible reader that in ancient times before the colonisation program of Europeans only blacks inhabited Africa then it would be foolish for us to think that in these lands white people lived or even Cauc-Asians made homes since this term more refers to Asians from the Caucasus regions so would not be an accurate term for white people genetically speaking. Would we describe the British people as Cauc-Asians? No, because they did not go to live in Britain from the Caucasus regions. They have descended from Anglo Saxons, Romans, Normans and including many other invading people.

20

Ancient Cushite soldiers

20

http://www.facebook.com/photo.php?pid=1894270&o=all&op=1&view=all&subj=4156
0148433&aid=-
1&id=1061939198&oid=41560148433#!/photo.php?pid=11590138&o=all&op=1&view
=all&subj=41560148433&aid=-
1&id=669290622&oid=41560148433&fbid=10150161470330623

When we apply the correct definitions then we will find the people we are looking for in ancient Israel. Only the uneducated can believe that black people can all turn white ignoring the fact that many today that claim to be Jews in Israel are really not the Semitic people of the land originally but European converts into Judaism.

We first look at Yosef who was taken into North-Africa (Egypt) and sold as a slave. Yosef was a handsome young black man. Notice that if you thought he was white you would be very wrong because when his brothers went to look for him they could not find him. One has to ask the question if ancient Egypt were Kematic black people then why would his brothers not find Yosef if he was a white skinned man? The reason is simple that he was not white but black and had mixed with the people so they could not find him.

> **Genesis 42:8** So Yosef recognized his brothers, but they did not recognize him.

Tracking a white man amongst the blacks would not be difficult especially one who is a foreigner. All they would have to do was to ask the locals if they have seen a white man and they would have spotted him like a sore thumb for sure because of the difference of his skin to theirs but we find no such thing even remotely happening even to the point his brothers do not recognise him which indicates to us that Yosef was black as were the other population and that he for all practical purposes looked like the locals. This is why the text goes to this length to tell you that he looked like the natives who were 'Black' so they could not recognise him.

Now let us examine another towering figure in the Bible of Moses. Moses as some of you may know was born in North Africa what today is referred to as Egypt to a black Hebrew family who were at that time dwelling amongst the Black Kematic people of Egypt. The Bible tells us the following details about Moses.

> **Exodus 2:1-2** And a man of the Beyth (house) of Lewi went and took as wife, a daughter of Lewi. **2** So the woman conceived, and bore a son: and when she saw that he was a beautiful child, she hid him three months.

The man here is Amram from the House of Lewi who went and took a daughter of Lewi whose name was Jochebed from the priestly tribe to be his wife. Jochebed then gave birth to a boy. Note the boy was called Moses by Pharaoh's daughter but Moses's parents gave him a different name. The name of Moses's father and mother are given in Exodus 6:20. However there is still detail missing here that the Bible is silent about which we learn elsewhere.

At this point in history Moses's parents were living in North-Africa in Egypt and it was decided by the King of Egypt that he was going to kill all the babies of the Hebrews that were male upon the advice of Balaam the son of Beor. Therefore when Moses was born his family hid him (Exo 2:3) however what is not given here is that Amram had decided not to have any more children and had send his wife away and separated from her for fear that if he had a child what was the point of putting his family's life in danger and of the child.

Sometimes many of us make similar choices but they are not always correct. When I left Islam I made a similar choice not to have any more children with my wife that if I was going to be persecuted for my faith how will I protect my wife and children and why put their life in danger. Just like Amram I also came to realise that this choice was wrong. Noakh had also thought of the same that YHWH is going to destroy the world then why should I even bother to marry until YHWH told him to go and marry and he married Naamah.

While the situation in Egypt was tense and dangerous Miriam, Moses's sister had a revelation that a saviour would be born for Israel and she then communicated this prophecy to her family which then brought about her father to call his wife back and to conceive the child Moses. Moses was then born with very high expectation of the nation for a deliverer as the prophecy was commonly known by the Hebrew Israelites that Elohim will send a deliverer. While popular folklore and modern movies depict Moses as a handsome white man but in fact he was a handsome black man as the text tells us the following.

Shemoth (Exo) 2:19 And they said, **A Mitzri (Egyptian)** delivered us from the hand of the shepherds, and he also drew enough mayim (water) for us, and watered the flock.

They said **an Egyptian** saved us? Did Moses show his passport and nationality or was it from his appearance that the girls concluded that he was an Egyptian?

Did Zipporah conduct an interview of Moses? No, therefore one can easily conclude based on the evidence supplied that people knew **the skin colour of the Egyptians was dark**. So what colour were the ancient Egyptians? Pick up any ancient source and you will find they were all black.

As a South-Easterner I can tell you instantly when I see a South-Indian or North-Indian because I can recognize them from the shading of the skin colour and I can even tell you the difference of a Chinese and Japanese so likewise Zipporah was not incorrect in her assumption to place him from Egypt though He was Hebrew. The bit of Moses being Hebrew was related to his culture while his colour was related to the region. In ancient times people were not discriminated by their colour but could be discriminated because of their culture as we know it happened to the Hebrews.

Now that we know the colour of ancient Egyptians we can see why all the films and pictures that show Moses as white are as false as the pictures that show Yahushua as white.

Deut 18:15 YHWH your Elohim will raise up unto you a Prophet from the midst of you, of your brethren, like unto me; you shall listen to him;

So if a prophet is raised up from amongst the BLACK people of Israel then what colour should that prophet be? These are the kind of details that many of you happily ignore but they cannot be ignored.

Deut 18:18 I will raise them up a Prophet from among their brethren, like unto you, and will put my words in his mouth; and he shall speak unto them all that I shall command him.

A prophet was going to be raised from amongst their brethren. All of you who think you have seen a white Jesus now should know what people will call you who know that he was not white. Since the brethren were Black and if it appeared that the prophet was white he would be rejected as a foreigner. Now you may understand why the European blue eyed 'Jesus' can never be accepted.

This should also explain why even some African nations like Nigeria which accept the white 'Jesus' are still in darkness because this person is not the original but the people have used him for profits and not spirituality. While the Master of the world is Black and yet to be given to these people and to be shown that the Master has a Torah that needs to be respected and obeyed. And if they do not obey it there will be eternal consequences.

King Solomon the wisest man of the East was the product of the union between King Dawud and Bathsheba. The Hebrew term Bat-Sheba means the daughter of Sheba. Let us examine this a little more who was Sheba to identify Bat-Sheba his daughter.

> **Beresheeth (Gen) 10:7** (HTHS) The sons of Cush were; Sheba, Chavilah, Sabtah, Raamah, and Sabtechah; and the sons of Raamah were Sheba and Dedan.

The Sheba mentioned in Genesis is the son of Cush. What colour were/are the Cushan people from Sudan? The Cushi people lived and still live in Sudan and upper and lower Nubian regions even today and I have shown you that Bathsheba King David's wife was an ancestor of these people and black in colour. Therefore now ask yourself what colour was the wisest man of the East King Solomon? **Can we really put down black people as unintelligent? Well history and the scriptures show that the wisest man to live was of very dark skin in fact black as black can be or black as coal because he was also the son of Tsiyon.**

Sheba and Dedan who were described as living in Northern Arabia regions were black.

George Rawlinson a 19th century European traveler, who passed through the region and described the Cha'b (also called in recent times Chub, Ka'ab, Kub) and Montefik bin Uqayl Arabs in Iraq and Khuzestan as "nearly black" and having the dark "copper" complexion of the "Galla Ethiopians" and other Abyssinians.

Thus we see that in the late 19th century, a group of Afro-Arabian tribes were well established and living in the region of Khuzestan, Iran and around the Persian Gulf as well as Basra, and the Shott al Arab in Iraq. There were known variously as Kaab, (Cha'ab or Chub), Kuleib, Al Muntafik (or Afek), Khuza'il, Khafajah, Uqayl or Aqil, and Jada.

Many of these men are the clearly documented descendants of the Beni Amir bin Sa'sa'a of the Hawazin bin Mansour. They were described until the 20th century as "near black" in color, tall and strongly built. In Iran they are called the "Tsiab". Many of their descendants live there even today still black in complexion.

This group of Black Iraqis are thus the remaining elements of the pure and original house of Arabia, which rose in ancient times from the Mountains of Ethiopia and migrated onto Iraqi and Khuzestan.

The Zenji of Basra

There was another smaller group of Black people, non-Muslims in out look and practice, who settled in Iraq as victims of forced labour otherwise known as slavery. They were known as the Zenji, from the land of Zanjnia (close to modern Tanzania). However it must be emphasized that there were also a great multitude of free Zenjis who had voluntarily settled in the Gulf.

---

[21] http://www.africaresource.com/rasta/sesostris-the-great-the-egyptian-hercules/the-black-iraqis-%E2%80%93-afro-arabian-mesopotamia-by-jide-uwechia/

The Zenji concentrated around Basra and lived co-harmoniously with their Arabian hosts. Some Zenjis worked on the plantations around Basra, doing the hard labour, while others were free traders and landowners. The Zenji took over Basra following an insurrection which took place in the mid-800s. The Zenji then ruled Basra for about 15 years, until the Islamic caliph sent troops. Many of the rebels were massacred, and others were sold to the Arab tribes.

Some under currents of racialism that one finds in present day Islamic societies developed from the fear and post traumatic stress of the reign of the Zenji in Iraq.

The Moors

Many other Black people in Iraqi came as sailors, traders, immigrants or pilgrims who decided to remain in Iraq. They came especially during the era of the Moorish Islamic Caliphate of Cordoba, Granada, and Egypt (i.e. the Fatimids).

Moors were Africans and Muslims of the Maghrib (also known as the western Sudan), who dominated Islam between the 9th and the 14th century and established a global empire reaching from Senegal to the shores of China.

Many of the Moors sailed in an ancient African ship called the dhow (or Arab dhow by western historians) which traditionally traveled the Mediterranean and Red sea coast of Africa on to Arabia, India and China.

Altogether there are more than 2 million black people in Iraq

It may come as a surprise that many Iranians were originally black also. Here is the image of King Darius who is mentioned in the Bible.

Note his hair is woolly which reveals to us that he looks like African men and carries similar type of hair style because all of the civilization started from Africa and spread out.

Additional proof

22

A Libyan, a Canaanite, a Syian, and a Nubian, bow to pharaoh. XVIIIth Dynasty

Note the features of the men which are all dark skinned, even the Canaanite the ancient name of Israel is of dark skin and not the typical Caucasian as incorrectly portrayed today.

23

Look at the pictures of the ancient people living in the Kanani region. Do they look Caucasian? No, they are all dark skin toned

---

[22] http://www.realhistoryww.com/
[23] http://www.realhistoryww.com/world_history/ancient/Canaan_1.htm

even the bottom right two are black as the painting tile has lost the dark colour on the face. Note the hair on all these people is braided such as African styles of hair. None of these people has Caucasian straight hair or will ever be classified Caucasian.

[24]Modern Indo-European languages - which include English - originated in Turkey about 9,000 years ago, researchers say.

A language family is a group of languages that arose from a common ancestor, known as the proto-language. Linguists identify these families by trawling through modern languages for words of similar sound that often describe the same thing, like water and wasser (German). These shared words - or cognates - represent our language inheritance.

According to the Ethnologue database, more than 100 language families exist. The Indo-European family is one of the largest families - more than 400 languages spoken in at least 60 countries - and its origins are unclear. The Steppes, or Kurgan theorists hold that the proto-language originated in the Steppes of Russia, north of the Caspian Sea, about 5,000 years ago.

The Anatolia hypothesis - first proposed in the late 1980s by Prof Colin Renfrew (now Lord Renfrew) - suggests an origin in the Anatolian region of Turkey about 3,000 years earlier. To determine which competing theory was the most likely, Dr Quentin Atkinson from the University of Auckland and his team interrogated language evolution using phylogenetic analyses - more usually used to trace virus epidemics.

Commenting on the paper, Prof Mark Pagel, a Fellow of the Royal Society from the University of Reading who was involved in earlier published phylogenetic studies, said: "This is a superb application of methods taken from

---

[24] http://www.realhistoryww.com/world_history/ancient/Anatolia_Turkey.htm

evolutionary biology to understand a problem in cultural evolution - the origin and expansion of the Indo-European languages. "This paper conclusively shows that the Indo-European languages are at least 8-9,500 years old, and arose, as has long been speculated, in the Anatolian region of what is modern-day Turkey and spread outwards from there." Their study is reported in Science.

Mapping the Origins and Expansion of the Indo-European Language Family

http://www.sciencemag.org/content/337/6097/957.abstract?sid=192102e8-a5bc-4744-ac5a-5500338ab381

Concerning Literature

Egyptians, Sumerians, Mohenjo-daroans, Harappans, and Cretans, Elamites, Anatolians, and Nubians, were literate 3,000 years, 4,000 years, who knows how many thousands of years, before the world ever heard of Greeks or Romans. And there is ample evidence of their literacy.

Yet there is not one single entry: describing any of the people of their times, whether it be friends, foes, or invaders: or even more incredulously, there is not one single entry describing invading Whites in any of their literature.

Contrast that with Greek and Roman writings, in which these NEWLY literate people, describe EVERYTHING and EVERYONE! The discrepancy is of course, not accidental, nor for lack of material.

Hopefully, the White man has simply withheld this material, and not destroyed it.

Ancient Europe

[25]CIVILIZATION OR BARBARISM: AN AUTHENTIC ANTHROPOLOGY BY CHEIKH ANTA DIOP (1981): PP. 15-16

The Grimaldi Negroids have left their numerous traces all over Europe and Asia, from the Iberian Peninsula to Lake Baykal in Siberia, passing through France, Austria, the Crimea, and the Basin of Don, etc. In these last two regions, the late Soviet Professor Mikhail Gerasimov, a scholar of rare objectivity, identified the Negroid type from skulls found in the Middle Mousterian period.

---

[25] http://www.realhistoryww.com/world_history/ancient/Minoan_Greece_1.htm

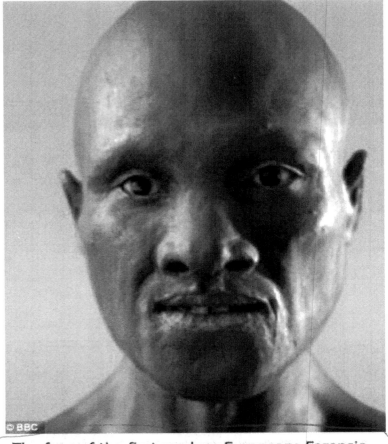

The face of the first modern European: Forensic scientist Richard Neave reconstructed the face based on skull fragments from 35,000 years ago found in the southwestern Carpathian Mountains of Romania in 2002-03. It was made for the BBC2 series The Incredible Human Journey.

This should be enough proof to prove that the ancient Europeans were not people of Caucasian skin colour in other words Albinos out of Africa which are a sub type of skin types.

[26]Modern White people

Please note: Modern White people have absolutely nothing to do with the following history. Though they are also Whites from central Asia (Albinos actually), just like the first Whites in Europe (who came circa 1,200 B.C.), they came at a much later date: circa 200 - 800 (A.D.). These modern people are the Germanics and Slavs, who were chased into Europe by the Huns of Asia. The last of these people, the Turks, were chased into the west by the Mongolians of Genghis Khan. Please see the Etruria-1 and Eastern Europe sections on the main menu for the history and genesis of those people.

Those modern Albinos who will acknowledge the ancient Blacks of Europe, encourage us to believe that the ancients were wiped-out, and the remaining absorbed by the Germanics, when they sacked Rome in 476. Romulus Augustus, the last Emperor of the Western Roman Empire, was deposed by Odoacer, a Germanic chieftain. In the East, the Byzantine end came when on April 2, 1453, Turkic Sultan Mehmed's army of some 80,000 men and large numbers of irregulars laid siege to the city of Constantinople. Despite a desperate last-ditch defense of the city by the massively outnumbered Christian forces, Constantinople finally fell to the Ottomans after a two-month siege on 29 May 1453. The last Byzantine Emperor, Constantine XI Palaiologos (though Byzantines were originally Greeks, by then, Slavs had made significant inroads), was last seen casting off his imperial regalia and throwing himself into hand-to-hand combat after the walls of the city were taken.

What the Albinos are trying to hide, is that Black rule in Europe lasted well after the medieval, and was only broken by the race wars, disguised by Albino historians as religious wars, of the 1600s. In continental Europe, these

---

[26] http://www.realhistoryww.com/world_history/ancient/Minoan_Greece_1.htm

were primarily the thirty years wars. In Britain there were many separate wars.

Note: As our knowledge increases we find more White lies as relates to ethnicity: The Franks and Frisians were native Black people. Undoubtedly in the future, we will find more White lies.

Germanic countries - Great Britain, Netherlands, Germany, Austria, Switzerland, Belgium, France, Spain, portugal, Scandinavians (Denmark, Sweden, Finland, Norway, Iceland, Faroe Islanders, not Sami).

The Slavs
Slavic peoples are classified geographically and linguistically into West Slavic (including Czechs, Kashubians, Moravians, Poles, Silesians, Slovaks and Sorbs), East Slavic (including Belarusians, Russians, Rusyns and Ukrainians), and South Slavic (including Bosniaks, Bulgarians, Croats, Macedonians, Montenegrins, Serbs and Slovenes).

Slavic countries - Russia, Ukraine, Poland, Greece, Hungary, Macedonia, Albania, Azerbaijan, Belarus, Bosnia and Herzegovina, Bulgaria, Croatia, Czech Republic, Hungary, Georgia, Kosovo, Moldova, Montenegro, Romania, Serbia, Slovakia, Slovenia, Estonia, Latvia, Lithuania.
Italy - mixed Slav/Germanic
Greece - Mixed, mostly Slav
Armenia - mixed Slav/Turk
Algeria - mixed Berber/Germanic
Tunisia - mixed Germanic/Berber

The Turks
Turkic peoples - Göktürks, Seljuks, Khazars (Jews), Mughals, Azerbaijani, Bashkir, Chuvash, Kazakh, Kyrgyz, Tatar, Uighur, Uzbek, and Sakha, Hephthalites.
Turkic Countries - Turkey, Azerbaijan, Kazakhstan,

Kyrgyzstan, Turkmenistan, Uzbekistan, Northern Cyprus (Turkish Republic of Northern Cyprus).

Countries with large populations of ethnic Turks and Turkic culture:
Turkey, Egypt, Iran, Libya, Iraq, Jordan, Kuwait, Lebanon, Oman, Qatar, Saudi Arabia, Syria, United Arab Emirates, Yemen, Bahrain.

[27]THE VANISHING EVIDENCE OF CLASSICAL AFRICAN CIVILIZATIONS by Prof. Manu Ampim

The widespread damage to the temple images has allowed Egyptologists to argue from such sources as the temple evidence that ancient Egypt was a multi-racial society and therefore belongs to the world's heritage and not necessarily to African history. There are probably about a million tourists each year who visit Egypt and Nubia, and they get a totally false view of the identity of the builders of these great civilizations, largely because the evidence of the builders' Black origin is disappearing. This vanishing evidence has enabled dishonest Egyptologists and tour guides to misrepresent the identity of the founders and builders of ancient Egypt by selectively pointing out the "non-African" images on the walls. Actually, the images which appear to look "non-African" have undergone a racial make-over and look nothing like they did originally. These images have been crudely recarved by European and Arab conspirators who work hard to eliminate all traces of African facial features. Only through exhaustive first-hand research can one demonstrate from the surviving on-site temple evidence that ancient Egypt was a Black civilization.

The altering of Black (African) facial features and the lightening of the skin colors of painted reliefs inside the tombs are central aspects of the conspiracy to destroy the

---

[27] http://www.realhistoryww.com/world_history/ancient/Minoan_Greece_1.htm

memory of classical African civilizations. The two main conspirator groups carrying out these acts are European and American research teams, and local government workers. Throughout Egypt and Nubia, the tomb images have suffered different levels of decay and destruction. In places such as Giza the tombs are closed as there is little left to see; in Tell Amarna the tomb carvings are in an advanced state of decay; in El Kab and Aswan many of the images have been systematically defaced; and in Beni Hassan only 4 of the 39 tombs are open because the rest are badly damaged. The only major location which has escaped serious tomb damage is Sakkara, but this may not remain true in the future because the conspirators' work is not complete, until they have destroyed or defaced all the evidence of classical African civilizations.

The problem of deterioration of the Kings Valley (KV) tombs has led to a growing international movement to build replica tombs and close the original structures. The tomb replication project will likely be implemented in the future. Under this plan, the popular tombs which have suffered irreparable damage, such as the tomb of Tutankhamen, will be permanently closed to the public. Once they are closed, the only persons who will have access to the original KV tombs will be Egyptian government officials and workers, and "qualified" researchers. The completion of this tomb replication project will be a major step in further erasing the memory of a Black Egypt. These replica tombs, with the lightened colors and remade facial features, will graphically demonstrate that the evidence of classical African civilizations is vanishing. This of course, holds true for the Minoan and all other Black civilizations.

[28]*Example of the White mans handiwork*

(Note the Libyan and Asiatic are depicted as White) Next page

---

[28] http://www.realhistoryww.com/world_history/ancient/Minoan_Greece_1.htm

98

Four peoples of the world: a Libyan, a Nubian, an Asiatic, and an Egyptian.
An artistic rendering by Heinrich von Minutoli (1820),
based on a mural from the tomb of Seti I

The ACTUAL tomb painting below

Tomb of Sety I - Book of Gates, fourth division (P)/fifth hour (H), beginning.

[29] According to the researcher, David Robl: The original story of the <u>Tower of Babel</u>, may describe the last phase of the building of the great temple for the god Enki at Eridu, (biblical Babel). Which was begun in this Uruk Period { this is the archaeological era, which has been argued as being the time immediately following the biblical Great Flood}.

The Tower of Babel

It was in this era, that a massive platform was built over the original shrine of Enki, and the building of a new temple begun, on top of this platform. This was the first platform-temple to be built in Mesopotamia, and the prototype of the later stepped platform-temples which we know as the Ziggurats. When finished, it towered above the surrounding countryside, and was certainly a major architectural innovation. Robl believes that the biblical king Nimrod, son of Cush, was in fact king Enmerkar.

---

[29] http://www.realhistoryww.com/world_history/ancient/Sumer_Iraq_1a.htm

Hanging Gardens of Babylon, an engraving by Martin Heemskerck
depicts the Tower of Babel in the background.

He continues: Cush (biblical son of Ham and grandson of
Noah), fathered Nimrod, who was the first potentate on
earth. Hence the saying, 'Like Nimrod a mighty hunter in
the eyes of Yahweh'.

Biblically, the mainstays of Nimrods Empire were Babel,
Erech and Akkad (Agade), all of them in the land of Shinar.
Shinar is (biblical ancient Sumer), Akkad was the capital of
the later Akkadian empire, (that city is still to be located).
Biblical Erech is Uruk, and Babel, as we have seen,
originally referred to Eridu.

But Nimrod himself has always eluded identification - until
now. The trick was to realize that the element 'kar' in
Enmerkar was the Sumerian word for 'hunter'. Thus the
name consists of a nomen plus an epithet - Enmer 'the
hunter'. This was precisely the epithet in Genesis, used to
describe Nimrod.

The next step was straightforward. Ancient Hebrew was
originally written without vowels (as in the Dead Sea
Scrolls). Vowel indicators were only added to the
Masoretic manuscripts, from the 5th century A.D, onwards.

So in early copies of Genesis the name Nimrod would simply have been written "nmrd". The name Enmer would also have been transcribed into Hebrew as 'nmr' - identical to Nimrod but for the last 'd'.

The Bible is well known for its play on words. Hebrew writers often translated foreign names into familiar Hebrew words, which they felt had appropriate meaning. In this case, they changed Sumerian 'nmr' to Hebrew 'nmrd', because the latter had the meaning 'rebel' - a perfect description for the king who defied God, by building a tower up to heaven.

Chapter 5
Yahushua is Black

It may not surprise you much after what you have read so far that Yahushua was indeed black, a man with woolly hair and bronze skin. He was not blond, white with blue eyes. This is the false photo that was created of him by the Europeans that has been making its rounds in many churches. The majority of the ancient churches still carry Yahushua's photo as a black man then why the charade by Western Christianity?

This is because they could not see Elohim being black. How could He be black since in the western minds black is inferior. The whole idea of slavery was born out of the notion that blacks are inferior beasts and can be enslaved. This was used to justify slavery while the African people had been cultured for thousands of years just look at the pyramids but the opposite scales the white races were still backward. The Greeks revered the blacks and took their wisdom from the black people and then just coloured it as their own. As stated earlier in this book the first real doctor was black who performed many operations.

Notice also that the Arabs used blacks to build up their armies the Berbers and Moors invaded Europe to conquer Spain and then left a lasting influence on architecture and science and even in English names. Today the name Moor is actually a family name that can be traced to the Moors who were Black. As you will read the Moors were a warrior class of people and in no time demolished all the forces of European Spain. This should give us a glimpse of North African warrior class who were exceptional fighters very seasoned. African people have generally known to be natural fighters just look in the boxing world how many boxers are Black and very good boxers.

In Africa there were tribes that had fighters that could kill lions with bare hand to hand combat. That should remind us of another person who had many African ancestors who would kill many with bare hands the man Samson. He was indeed black with locks of hair and as has been shown only black folks have locks. White people do not have locks in their hair naturally.

[30]The conquest of the former Roman province of Hispania by the Moors (note that "Moors" only means the people from the northwest corner of Africa who carried out the conquest, including both Arabs and the original natives, the Berbers) marked the history and culture of Portugal and particularly Spain profoundly. This is the story of the Moorish invasion and occupation.

In April 711, the Arab governor of Tangiers, Tariq ibn-Ziyad, crossed the strait between what are now Morocco and Spain with an army of nine or ten thousand Berbers (the place where they landed was soon to have a new name, the rock of Tariq, Jabal Tariq — Gibraltar). Goth King Roderick hastily took an army south, but Táreq and his Berber troops defeated it in a battle near the River Guadalete, and the king himself was never seen again except in legend.

Tariq ordered that a group of prisoners be cut into pieces and their flesh boiled in cauldrons, and then released the rest, telling them to spread the word about Moorish practices. He and his army then followed the old Roman roads north to the Goths' capital city, Toledo, pausing only to take the cities of Éjica and Córdoba. Resistance was slight, whether reduced by Tariq's intimidatory propaganda or not.

The invasion had been ordered by Musa, the governor of Ifriquiyya (North Africa), and the following year, General Musa himself landed with another Berber army of 18,000, which this time included a large number of Arab officers. He took Medina Sidonia, Seville and Mérida, where a last stand by the Goths failed. And that was more or less that. While on their flanks subordinates took care of Portugal and the east of Spain, Tariq and Musa met up in Toledo and continued north-east up the Ebro valley, encountering practically no resistance at all.

How were armies which at no point exceeded a total of forty thousand troops able to conquer a territory with a

---

[30] http://spainforvisitors.com/archive/features/moorishinvasion.htm

population estimated at around four million, and in so brief a time? Historians have different answers. To begin with, the Goths were a ruling class which had never mixed with or been accepted by its subjects, and it seems clear that the Hispano-Roman population did nothing to support them and in most cases welcomed the invaders. In addition, they were far from united themselves: the Goths had a tradition of parricide and fratricide which makes Caligula look like the son you always wanted. Roderick himself had been crowned after a civil war, and many of his opponents simply took sides with the Moors (it is not unlikely that one of the initial reasons for the Moorish invasion was an invitation from supporters of Prince Achila, Roderick's rival for the throne. The Achila band, the theory goes probably thought that the Moors would come, defeat Roderick, grab some booty and go home).

The Moors proved to be more politically skilful than the ousted Goths, as well. For example, they bribed landowners - including Goth aristocrats and Christian clergy - into cooperation by allowing them to keep their properties. In addition, some historians sustain that there may have been mass conversion to Islam - after all, the difference between one monotheistic religion and the next is not all that important, especially at a time when the element being stressed in both is the existence of an omnipotent god. Under the Visigoths (Goths of the West), the tax burden was heavy and although the special taxes the Muslims imposed on Christians and Jews were more bearable, peasants were better off and had more freedom as Muslims, while serfs became freemen on conversion. Jews, on the other hand, did not even need to change their faith to find themselves relieved of the oppression they were accustomed to under Christian rule.

It may be shocking to learn this but European Spain was ruled for over 800 years by Blacks, yes black people from North Africa. Even though these Black people had been forced into Islam before the invasion of Spain but they were cultured and were into the arts and sciences and they allowed these principles to flourish in Spain. They had beautiful architectures built and science

105

flourished in medieval Spain which before this was stuck in medieval superstition and cultic practices.

Below is an ancient painting of Miriam and the son Yahushua called Jesus in modern vernacular which is a foreign name to the Bible. Look at both the son and the mother and their colour is black. One more thing as you can see the Popes specially stood in front of and prayed to the Black Madonna while telling the world to pray to the white Madonna they had carved up to fool the people into idolatry while themselves prayed to the black picture of Miriam who they considered gave them real spirituality. They had hid these things from the world to hide Miriam and Yahushua's real identity from the world. It was on the order of the Popes that all the black Madonna's were removed from public viewing and replaced with the European modern art of Miriam in white which is a totally false picture of her and her Son.

31

http://www.facebook.com/photo.php?pid=1894270&o=all&op=1&view=all&su

You see even the Pope knew and bowed before the real Black Yahushua and Miriam and not against a white one.

This painting above is Polish and it's called "Matka Boska Czestochowska" also known as "the Black Madonna." This information came from a well wisher from Poland who told me that even Polish people know that the real Messiah and Miriam are not white.

Let me show you a clearer one in which you can see that Yahushua is indeed looking like an African man.

The Black Virgin of Montserrat: a copy at Barcelona Cathedral
The original is said to have been make by St. Luke in 54 A.D.

bj=41560148433&aid=-
1&id=1061939198&oid=41560148433#!/photo.php?pid=31010145&o=all&op=
1&view=all&subj=41560148433&aid=-
1&id=1062825316&oid=41560148433&fbid=1390154628223

[32]Many images of the Black Madonna still exist today. Ean Begg reports the existence at one time or another of 450, mostly in Europe, and Marie Durand-LeFebvre reported on 272, mostly in France. Following are listed those images of the Black Madonna which according to reports still exist, are still black and can still be seen. Many more are found in the literature but some were destroyed during the French Revolution and religious wars, some have disappeared or are in private collections, a few have been lightened or repainted and are no longer black and still others are copies of the more famous Black Madonna's such as those of Le Puy or Guadalupe. They are not included in this list.

Does the baby look Caucasian?

Ancient Ysraelites

---

[32] http://campus.udayton.edu/mary/resources/blackm/blackm.html

Captives taken by the Assyrians

Notice the picture above with the twelve disciples. What colour are they?

One simple question to solve Yahushua's culture and colour one can use to inquire that if Yahushua was not black then why paint Him and His mother black? Why would Luke who was a Levite (See my book Beyth Yahushua, The Son of Tzadok, The Son of Dawud) be describing Yahushua as black if Yahushua was of Caucasian skin colour? Some Pastors and preachers ask what is the point in whether He was black or white and that we should only be concerned about the salvation of the people.

If Abbah YHWH made Him a human being then there is a great point in us knowing what culture and colour He was born into and what colour and ethnicity He was in order to identify His people. Yahushua was born in North Africa then why would a white Yahushua be strolling around today as He does in the paintings of Europe. They are nothing but false pictures with no value to them.

Below is one of them which is entirely false.

Yahushua came for His people who were Hebrew Israelites so if you can't even define Yahushua then how can you know who are Hebrews today?

Even an Egyptian Gamal Abdul Nasser a Former President of Egypt said in 1956 that He could not respect the present Jews because they left Israel black and came back white. One can see why such a comment even arose in hostilities with Israel by a Muslim. So was the Muslim President lying? No, he was telling the truth of history but will you see it?

It's of paramount importance to understand Yahushua and His culture to go and search for the lost sheep of the House of Israel the ten Northern tribes which many are still living in the African continent and also migrated across to the other nations as slaves taken into Europe and America.

Our Father YHWH did not just wave a wand and say to Yahushua to remain invisible to the world. The point is that He was given a colour, a family and a heritage. It would be foolish to deny any of this. While those who see white images of Yahushua and His disciples I personally would reject outright as liars and you have plenty of them in Christianity believe me I have met them. The family of Yahushua were in a certain location of the world called North Africa and they were not going to turn up as a white family in Times Square, New York or the Trafalgar Square in London feeding pigeons. It is high time we remove the deception and be very clear who it is we serve and what He means to all of us faithful to Him.

33

[33] http://campus.udayton.edu/mary/resources/blackm/blackm02.html#fra

Here is a painting that has been restored in Ethiopia of Miriam and Yahushua.

34

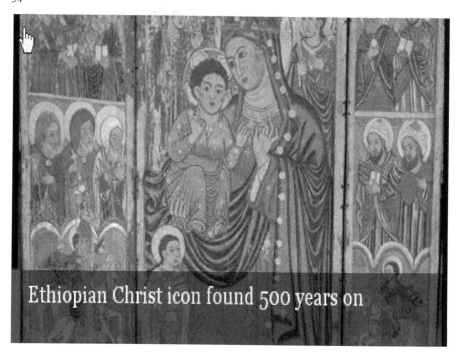

Ethiopian Christ icon found 500 years on

No matter how much the Caucasian liars cover up trying to make Miriam look white the baby can be clearly seen to exhibit woolly hair which only exists in African people. In fact in reality both the mother and child are black. What a shame the lies that are propagated in Churches daily!

Here is a close-up of the baby. No white child has hair like this.

---

[34] www.ethiopian-news.com

Unfortunately the cover-up to hide the identity of Yahushua is far and wide and many Christian people still carry the false doctored pictures in their homes which are simply idolatries of a bygone age while we are forbidden to create images of things in heaven but these images created by non-Israelites at least show us what Yahushua really looked like.

Here is a coin of the Black Messiah that no one can mistake what He looked like.

35

Byzantine Empire, Andronicus II & III, Joint reign 2 February 1325 - 24 May 1328 A.D.

The faces of Christ and the emperors are well struck and clear on the reverse, which is rare on this very crudely struck type.

Here is a close up of the face.

[35] http://www.forumancientcoins.com/catalog/roman-and-greek-coins.asp?vpar=681&pos=0#Byzantine%20Gold

114

Anyone can spot the African facial features here including the locks of hair that the Messiah has? This is the closest description of the Black Messiah we have as an adult.

I think at this point you would no doubt be very clear who the Messiah is and who it was that He came to save from being lost. While Christianity has much repenting to do themselves of their past lies and error the reality is that the true faith was of Hebrew Israelite origins and not called Christianity or Judaism. The truth is that in the first century there was no Christianity and no Judaism. Judaism as we know it today was created as a religion in 66 CE just before the destruction of the Second Temple while Christianity as a religion was not created until later that same century.

The above coin is from the period of Justinian the Great during the 6th century CE. It shows the image of the Messiah with kinky hair as black people have it.

> **Act 11:26 (KJV)** And when he had found him, he brought him unto Antioch. And it came to pass, that a whole year they assembled themselves with the church, and taught much people. And <u>the disciples were called Christians first in Antioch.</u>

In the book of Luke a Levite Physician tells us that it was at Antioch that the Hellenists called the disciples Christians because before this the term was not used for the disciples and was not at least in existence for the disciples of Yahushua however there were people who were called Christians in the Greek lands but they were the worshippers of an Egyptians deity by the name of

Serapis. The original disciples were of Hebrew Israelite stock and carrying out the faith practices of their forefathers then it is evident that they were referred to as Netzarim or as Hebrew branches. This is the name that the Messiah Yahushua gave them in John 15:5.

> **John 15:5** I am the vine, <u>you are the branches</u>. He that abides in me, and I in him, the same brings forth much fruit: for without me you can do nothing.

One should be careful to what title is one called because today the term Christian is confused with Catholic, Anglicanism, Jehovah's witnesses, Mormonism and the various 38,000 denominations of Christendom that by large live lawlessly not practicing the Torah. We the faithful believers refuse to be addressed as Christians and would rather be referred to as Netzari or Netzarim that is what the Master Yahushua called us and that is what we call ourselves.

Chapter 6
The First Rastafarian - Samson of the Bible

Samson who was the strongest man that has ever lived is mostly depicted as a white Caucasian but nothing could be further from the truth. His appearance both in movies and in the real world is nothing like what he was. Actually Samson was a very ordinary black guy. We are told in the Babylonian Talmud Sotah 10a that Samson was lame in his feet. He became strong every time the Ruakh Ha Kadosh or the Spirit of the Most High came upon him.

> **Shoftim (Judges) 14:5** Then went Shimshon (Samson) down, and his father and his mother, to Timnath, and came to the vineyards of Timnath: and, behold, a young lion roared against him. **6** And the Ruakh (Spirit) of YHWH came mightily upon him, and he tore it apart as he would have torn a young goat, and he had nothing in his hand: but he told not his father or his mother what he had done.

I will prove here to you that Samson was black with dreadlocks just like Rastafarians today. In fact he was asked not to cut them ever because it is through these that His strength flowed and enabled him to subdue even a 1000 men or to tear a lion apart with his bare hands. I have seen many strong men but I can tell you that I have seen no such feats by the strongest in the West but Samson was a different category altogether a very ordinary looking man that became extremely strong that would put to shame the most trained men in the West who claim to be strong because YHWH's Spirit was upon Him.

Although there are many strong men around the world and have been in history but the class of strength exhibited by the Hebrew Israelites is unparalleled by any in history.

> **Gen 30:5-6** And Bilhah conceived, and bore Yaqub a son. **6** Then Rach'el said, Elohim has judged my case, and He has also heard my voice, and given me a son: therefore she called his name Dan.

Bilhah was Rachel's maid who was Laban's daughter given over to Jacob as wife and Bilhah gave birth to Dan. I will prove it here that all the tribe of Dan was Black because Bilhah was a Black woman married to a man with African ancestors that are Jacob and his father in law Laban who became an Aramaen and was an albino, which is why his name tells us in Hebrew that he was 'white.' This was not common but he though from a black family turned out white as often happens in Africa.

According to the rabbinic traditions and the Targum of Jonathan Gen. R. lxxiv. 14, Bilhah was one of the daughters of Laban. If this is true then we can see the same pattern of kinship in the family line of Laban as we see in Abraham. Laban had at least two wives and two concubines one which was given to him was the daughter Bilhah and the other was Zilpah, they were twins born to his wife Adinah.

The book of Jasher tells us the following: *30:13 And Laban had no sons but only daughters, and <u>his other wives.</u>* This proves my thesis is correct. He did get sons later because of Jacob's increases. Beor was the son born to Laban and should ring a bell because he was indeed African and black. One of his sons Bela who is mentioned in the book of Jasher which you can purchase from the www.african-israel.com website with commentary and read the history missing in the book of Genesis. He was from a region in ancient times called Dinhabah which is the modern city in Tanzania called Anabah (Jasher 57:41) and this was ruled by the king of Africa, this man Bela was crowned king over Esav's people (Jasher 57:42). Well unless you are going to tell me Tanzania is inhabited by white Europeans it is in fact part of Africa and has black people. Also note the original inhabitants of Australia the aborigines are from Tanzania and you can go check their colour to verify what I have said is true and factual and not just conjecture.

We can trace this using kinship analysis to point out where these ladies came from or who was their father or grandfather. Bilhah names her firstborn son Dan and Zilpah names her son Gawd. Many people in modern times confuse this with the term God as a false deity name. There is no ancient deity by the name of God but in ancient times there were towers erected to serve false gods and as such the term is derived from migdol which means a prominent tower and the Hebrew term G-d or Gawd is a derivative of this.

118

So one can see Samson was a black judge mighty in strength. The tribes in Ethiopia or the Beta Yisrael identify themselves with the tribe of Dan and they are all black. Contrary to popular belief the Danish are not Danites. This is a popular folklore more than anything else there is no real connection between them and the real Hebrews of Dan.

The term בלהה has the same sound and close association with a word in our language or Urdu from the Aramaic script called Balah which means something that scares or frightens you. This is why the Hebrew of Bilhah does not mean as many attest timid. This is a modern definition.

It in fact means one that unleashes terror. The Hebrew word used for terror is Behelah and has close associations with this term. The other term Balah in Hebrew means 'to wear out' so the combination of these tells me the correct meaning of Bilhah is what I described above. We know this is the meaning because the term Belial is a derivative of this word which means the 'prince of demons' and what do demons generally do? If you saw one they would instil terror in you, you will not be smiling but running for your life. The ancient Hebrew picture of this word is a house, a picture of a lion and two feathers which indicates this shows a house of strength or one that contains strength.

The tribe of Dan were the tribe of Judges as law makers one's who made sure YHWH's law was followed. When Samson would have walked the streets people would have been extremely scared of this very strong man because he had no match in the land so one can see why names in Hebrew culture have meanings behind them to personal character and traits. Genesis 29:2 tells us that the family of Laban controlled water resources as his daughter was near a well when Jacob first saw her.

Genesis 29:5 Then he said to them, do you know Laban the **son of Nachor**? And they said, we know him.

Nachor was the son of Terach but was also the name of Terach's father.

119

Bilhah was also the most favourite wife of Jacob after Rachel and he loved her dearly. She was also a very good woman who looked after the young of Rachel after she died.

> **Judges 13:5** For, lo, you shall conceive, and bear a son; and no razor shall come on his head: for the child shall be a Nazarite to Elohim from the womb: and he shall begin to deliver Y'sra'el out of the hand of the Plushtim (Philistines).

So Samson was commanded not to cut his locks which typically would look like a Rastafarian's head. He was called a Nazarite. These had to restrict for a certain time under vow not to cut hair or drink alcohol but in Samson's case his vow was meant to be permanent for life, imagine how long would be his hair if he never cut it. We are told in Lamentations the following.

> **Lam 4:7** Her Nazarites were purer than snow, they were whiter than milk, they were more of mahogany in body than rubies, their polishing was of sapphire

The Nazarites were purer than snow is not a comparison of their complexion but of their inner-being. The whole point of a Nazarite was to take an oath to serve YHWH and not to cut their hair for a certain time and not to consume alcohol. So the purity of purer than snow suggested here is the quality of their inner self or their devotion to YHWH was pure and YHWH recognises that.

> **Lam 4:8** Their visage is **blacker than a coal**…

Lot of people assume from verse 7 that this is talking about white people but it is not. It is talking about Blacks who have a mahogany complexion which is translated as red in many bibles. Verse 8 clarifies further that they are Black. Some Black people do have a mahogany look and we find this in many ancient Egyptian paintings the faces of black people having a red hue. Note the parallel of verse 7 with Nazarite. Samson was a black man and the truth needs to be told far and wide. It was not only for Samson but the rest of the majority of the Hebrews too. We are told in Numbers.

> **Numbers 6:2-5** Speak unto the children of Y'sra'el, and say unto them, When either man or woman shall separate

120

themselves to vow a vow of a Nazarite, to separate themselves unto YHWH: **5** All the days of the vow of his separation there shall no razor come upon his head: until the days be fulfilled, in the which he separates himself unto YHWH, he shall be set-apart, and **shall let the _LOCKS_ of the hair of his head grow**.

Note this commandment was given to both men and women so the locks once again mentioned show us that the majority of Israelites were of woolly hair like the African people today.

If this does not convince you then let me give you more to chew on.

> **Judges 14:1** And Shimshon (Samson) went down to Timnath, and saw a woman in Timnath of the daughters of the Plushtim (Philistines).

Samson fell in love with a woman from the Philistines. Well a black man will obviously likely fall in love with a black woman. The Philistines were a people of colour.

> **Genesis 10:13-14** And Mitzrayim (Egypt) begot Ludim, Anamim, Lehabim, Naphtuhim, **14** Pathrusim, and Casluhim from who came the Plushtim (Philistines), and Caphtorim.

The Philistines were the sons of Mitzrayim (Egypt) and they were **black**.

> **Judges 14:5-6** Then went Shimshon (Samson) down, and his father and his mother, to Timnath, and came to the vineyards of Timnath: and, behold, a young lion roared against him. **6** And the Ruach (Spirit) of YHWH came mightily upon him, and he tore it apart as he would have torn a young goat, and he had nothing in his hand: but he told not his father or his mother what he had done.

History is witness that the only people who have been recorded as tearing a strong Lion with their bare hands happened amongst the African people. This gives us another clue to the identity of Samson.

Judges 16:17-19 That he told her all his heart, and said to her, There has not come a razor upon my head; for I have <u>been a Nazarite to Elohim from my mother's womb</u>: if I be shaven, then my strength will go from me, and I shall become weak, and be like any other man. **18** And when Delilah saw that he had told her all his heart, she sent and called for the princes of the Plushtim (Philistines), saying, Come up this once, for he has showed me all his heart. Then the princes of the Plushtim (Philistines) came up to her, and brought money in their hand. **19** And she made him sleep upon her knees; and she called for a man, and she caused him to **shave off the seven braids** of his hair; and she made him vulnerable, and his strength left him.

Note Samson had never had a haircut and his hair was in braids or locks. Only Africans have locks. Based on Hebrew Israelites customs and the story of Samson the Rastafarians do not like to cut their hair comparing it on inner spirituality and the strength of a man which does indeed connect with Samson's story. Note also unless you go and artificially make braids these only occur naturally amongst the Africans. The Rastafarian word started from the Emperor of Ethiopia who came to rule as Haile Selessie calling himself with the title the Lion of Judah with his cousin in 1930 whose name was Ras Tafari (Ras means governor and Tafari is a region in Ethiopia). This is confirmed by the Hebrew Israelite scholar Kohen Michael Ben Levi in his book "Israelites and Jews page 78."

The Rastafarian movement took their title from the emperor of Ethiopia and they are right in believing that the original Hebrews were Black and the chosen of YHWH Elohim. They are not wrong to keep their locks and are likely the direct descendants of Hebrew Israelites worldwide. YHWH will one day restore them back with all of Israel as He has promised and even prophesied that even if they die in their places of abode He will raise them and take them back to their original land (Ezek 37). This prophecy in Ezekiel has never been fulfilled yet and we await its fulfilment.

What most people today do not know is that the ancient people this includes the Babylonians, the Persians and even many of the Greeks were of colour. Even if you look at ancient Europe you will find black people here.

The original Arabs were black because these were people who migrated from the Western and Northern African regions to go and settle in what is today known as Arabia. Saudi Arabia or Arabia in general is centred in the land of Africa and should properly be called North Eastern Africa which is why the African people freely moved and lived there in the ancient days.

Africa in the Bible

Ophir is the biblical term for the land of Africa noting that the term 'Africa' is of late historical derivative. In the Greek tongue the term Frike means cold and horror and appending the A to it becomes Africa which means not the land of cold and horror but as can be seen many horrors were perpetrated there by the so called civilised nations of the world one such as slavery and colonization to subjugate the 10,000 kingdoms that existed there. In Latin language the term Africa meant sunny. It is also well known that India's and China's ancestors were Africans.

Many people have already decided that all the Africans are the sons of Ham. If you have come to this conclusion also then this is fairly inaccurate and very misleading. Let me show you something in the bible again.

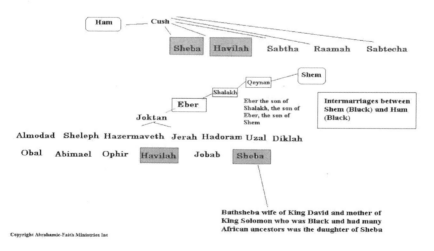

These are the genealogies mentioned in Genesis chapter 10 for Ham and Shem the two sons of Noakh. Notice that in most of your bibles one son of Shem is missing called Qeynan who was the father of Shalakh, the father of Eber so this Qeynan is the connection to Abraham being of Black skin colour.

If you look in the above picture one of Cush's great granddaughters was Bathsheba who was married to King David so a line goes directly from King David a black king to Cush who was also black, hence this is why King Solomon was also of Black colour. King David was not Caucasian but black of Negroid features. He is described in the Bible as red-black incorrectly translated in the KJV bible as ruddy. Many are therefore confused to think this man must be white in fact he was not and this is how the deception is perpetuated on good people.

> **First Shema'el (Sam) 17:42** And when the Philistine looked about, and saw Dawud, he disdained him: for he was but a youth, and of **reddish-black appearance**, and of a fair countenance.

Eber the son of Shalakh, the son of Qaynan, the son of Shem had two sons one was called Peleg and one Joktan. One of Joktan's sons was Ophir and it is mainly from him that we get the modern term Africa or the ancient term Afri. Ophir inhabited the African continent while not forgetting genetic land mass of Y'sra'el is also in Africa and not in the middle-east which is a 20th century word concocted by the British in 1928. We are told in the Bible that King Solomon the black king sent expeditions to Ophir which is modern day Africa to bring back gold to show that he had ties with the various kingdoms in Africa and why wouldn't he since he himself was black of African stock since Y'sra'el was one kingdom in Africa.

> **First Kings 9:28** And they came to *OPHIR*, and fetched from there gold, four hundred and twenty talents, and brought it to king Sulahmon.

Here Ophir refers to Africa about which was a region shared by Havilah for which we are told that the gold there is good (Gen 2:11).

Keturah was Joktan's daughter and married to Abraham while Joktan is the true progenitor of the Arab race one of the first to

124

inhabit Arabia parts of the region were freely travelled to and shared by ancient Africa.

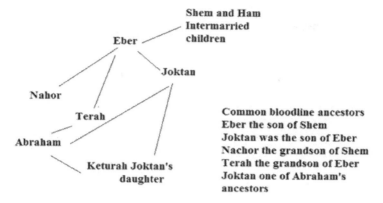

Now it should make sense that Yahushua the Messiah is called the Son of Abraham in Matthew's genealogy 1.1. Abraham was also a man of colour and not white as falsely depicted in movies alongside Moses and Yahushua. His wife Sarah was from a well known African clan though the daughter of Haran she was titled Sarai which translated my princess actually refers to a people in Africa called Sara, living in Chad. Note YHWH appends the H to her name making it Sarah. She was also a black woman.

Is Colour and race important?

One question that continues to fester is about colour and race. On one discussion with a black Hebrew the argument went something like this, "Colour does not matter it's of no consequence and Yah did not choose us because we were of black colour." Then the following scripture is quoted to defend the irrelevance of colour.

> **Debarim (Deuteronomy) 7:7-8** YHWH did not set his love upon you, nor choose you, because you were more in number than any people; for you were the fewest of all people: **8** But because YHWH loved you, and because he would keep the oath which he had sworn unto your ahvot (fathers), has YHWH brought you out with a mighty hand, and redeemed you out of the Beyth (house) of slavery, from the hand of Pharaoh King of Mitzrayim (Egypt).

I want to set forth an important point. The Most High El YHWH created only in one colour. This does sound radical and shocking but this is reality.

That is right he only created in one colour and that was BLACK and from that one colour all the other colours came out. When we examines history accurately then we discover that most races had a common black ancestor, like the Chinese, the Japanese moors, the Indians, the Aztecs, even the European ancestors were blacks, etc, etc. This creation in black colour was not about superiority but what was being revealed. The first man Adam was in the likeness of Adam Kadmon or the prototype of man who is also the Messiah Yahushua. So what colour is Adam Kadmon?

It is a known fact that the human colour black has more melanin or pigmentation. So when you see other colours all you are seeing is less of the pigmentation melanin. If you start removing the pigmentation from skin it starts to change shades to dark brown light brown to white etc.

However, many of us like to believe that colour does not matter then why is it that throughout history people have used colour to persecute those of non-white colour?

The truth is that the black colour was thought of as inferior by the general populations in the West and even in the east where in the Asian sub-continent they use creams like Fair and Lovely to improve skin colour, bleaching products in Nigeria and Kenya how to get rid of the darker skin. Have you ever wondered why? This is because it was the choice of the Creator which Satan hates and Satan reflects his hatred through people. He is not going to stand in the public square and show you his hatred, he is a spiritual being and in order to manifest himself he still has to possess a human body.

Apart from Hitler's hatred of the European Jews did he not hate the blacks? Before we all start to hate Hitler we need to understand he was fighting what he saw as the Zionist threat against his nation of ruthless bankers who wanted to control financial affairs in Germany.

Today the Zionist control major financial institutions for good or bad, more bad then good. Some of them known in the guise of IMF and World Bank. I judge no man but my job is to present the facts but I leave the judging to the Creator Elohim.

This disinformation campaign that the Zionist media does is nothing new under the sun that they learnt from their American compatriots who fuel the fire by supplying the planes, bombs that then kill innocent civilians all funded by uncle Sam. Uncle Sam was also caught red handed when they were doing the same thing to the Black Americans through what is called CoIntelpro (Counter Intelligence FBI) and Black Boule (A Masonic fraternity with Top black people selected to disinherit their own people, promote false values and discredit the Black Negroes who are part of the true Israelite tribes so they can never rise up. These Blacks who join the Black Boule are the ones who get favours and they have to swear initiation oaths, do homosexuality so that if they ever want out they can be persecuted, ridiculed as liars. For doing this they can get power and wealth. Many Blacks in the Hollywood film industry, the Church scene are part of this charade. Their core objective is so that the Blacks never rise up with a Messiah figure. The ones controlling the Blacks are of course some of the Caucasian elitist who fear the Blacks.

One of the targets is black Negro individuals they feared a messiah being raised in their midst. Dr Martin Luther King was their target, read between the lines who killed him. The question is why? Is it because the Negro's are the real chosen people? Think about it.

Did not the Caucasian people bring the Black Africans into slavery and boasted of their superior colour? It's always about maintaining white supremacy in some guise believe it or not.

I have heard many Caucasians say today that they are superior as they have made all the technological advances so is that not colour boasting? When we know the western civilizations advances only amount to the destruction of the planet and not for the greater good which was given to Y'sra'el to bring forth.

127

Then one must ask can we use the scripture I gave you above (Deut 7:7-8) to say that Elohim does not care about colour. We would all like to think that in YHWH's eyes we are equal but even then did not YHWH set a standard for equality? Look what he said in the same chapter as I quoted above to show the inadequacy of those who do not know how to tackle the issue of colour and simply detract foolishly by saying that colour is of no consequence. The black colour defined Adam our ancient father and our mothers Chava and others.

Let me now show you something in the ancient most Hebrew script. Her name is Chava which appears as follows: Khet, Yud and Heh חוה.

The modern Hebrew picture is meaningless and tells us nothing but let us look at the ancient Hebrew picture to understand it's real meaning.

The first character Khet reveals to us the whole picture with the meaning of Concealment, of Darkness and of the Bosom. Chava was black this is identified in the khet the first letter of her name. In Ancient Hebrew contrary to popular error that many teachers teach Hebrew was a monosyllable language and not a two or three letter roots as believed. One character defines the word and the rest gives shape to the word in further explanation. So these pictures mean Black or dark living creature of beauty like a bird. Is it ironic that in the British and some other cultures the slang term "bird" came to signify a beautiful woman. The analogy actually goes back to our mother Chava who had the character Wah which signifies the feather in the ancient text and not the description "nail" or "tent peg" which is a later development

.

> **Debarim (Deuteronomy) 7:1-3** When YHWH your Elohim shall bring you into the land where You go in to possess it, and He has cast out many nations before you, the Hittites, and the Girgashites, and the Amorites, and the Canaanites, and the Perizzites, and the Hivites, and the Yebusites, seven nations greater and mightier than You; **2** And when YHWH your Elohim shall deliver them before

you; You shall conquer them, and utterly destroy them; You shall make no covenant with them, nor show mercy unto them: **3** <u>Neither shall You make marriages with them</u>; your daughter You shall not give unto his son,[36] nor his daughter shall You take unto your son.

Read carefully what YHWH said that the Y'sraelites were not allowed to make marriages with the seven nations mentioned in Debarim 7:1. They were not allowed to mingle or to produce offspring with them. Historically we know all these seven nations were black and so were the Hebrews so YHWH forbid for them to mingle. Consequently one may assume that colour does not matter but actually colour and race both matter. YHWH's non-allowance to marry was inevitably for reasons of both race and colour. He did not want the children of Y'sra'el to have children from idolater nations and their customs but where do we see a strong condemnation where colour comes into play?

When YHWH judged Y'sra'el it was always typically in the colour of white. This is an important factor and let me show you.

> **We'Debar (Numbers) 12:1** And Miriam and Aharon spoke against Musa (Moses) because of the Cushite woman whom he had married: for he had married a Cushite woman. **9** And the anger of YHWH burned hot against them; and He departed. **10** And the cloud departed from off the tabernacle; and, behold, **MIRIAM BECAME LEPROUS, WHITE AS SNOW**: and Aharon looked upon Miriam, and,

It is important to note that YHWH judged Miriam for speaking against Moses and the Cushite black wife even though Miriam herself was black but there was another underlying issue which caused her to speak for which YHWH rebuked her and turned her white.

This is clear that white is the colour of judgment. If you can see it see that the colour white was used to judge the black Hebrews when they became slaves in the cross Atlantic slave trade to the

---

[36] It is forbidden to marry outside the community of believers who believe in the Messiah Yahushua.

129

Caucasian races. Next time someone says colour does not matter be careful Yahushua was Black therefore colour and race both matter though YHWH loves all colours as they all derived out of the Black colour first chosen for creation but His Son was not a white supremacist nor a white pacifist. Another reason why Yahushua was BLACK was because it shows he took the colour of the most abused race on our planet and identified with their sorrows, their pain and rejection (Isa 53:5). Did not the white people reject the Black man, despised them and scolded them? Yes and so was our Master despised, rejected and put down. Who were the Romans? They were Caucasian Mediterranean's who identified with the Italian race and they thought of themselves superior to all men. There are many books written about the Romans I advise you to read some.

Romans were not alone in doing this others did this too. I once had the pleasure of meeting and listening to the only Black Baroness Lady Benjamin Floella in London who described in stark details to the sitting audience how once when she was an eleven years old child in England she was looked down upon while waiting in shops they would not serve her first and made her wait and made rude remarks about her black skin in the 1950s Britain. Can you believe this happening to a child in the twentieth century? Yes I can understand white racist's minds though the Baroness has beautiful Black shiny skin how someone can make such remarks is all the more obvious to me is out of sheer contempt and hatred of the colour Black which was also the colour of our Saviour.

Those who say to you that colour does not matter then turn around and reject you for teaching truth proves the contradiction in such people's state of mind. If colour does not matter then why do they reject you as black Hebrews? Why can't they say that OK colour does not matter so if you believe many blacks were Hebrews its OK as this is your belief and I can live with that? How come they never say this? They usually say the reverse. This shows deep down in their psyche though they cannot admit nor understand colour does matter.

YHWH started this world with one Black man Adam then we see great cultures arose from the Black races, they built beautiful magnificent buildings like the pyramids and such things as hanging gardens of Babylon the ancient wonders of the world things that we do not even comprehend today while when Israel became a nation and sinned by not obeying Torah YHWH struck them down and they became slaves to the white races. Look around you where the Hebrews are today and who are their masters? I guarantee you it will be a Western nation. However when the cycle completes of the six thousand years then Yahushua the Black Messiah will return and we the Black Hebrews will rise back to glory and a superb Kingdom. So you need to know we are in a cycle and our status is about to be changed by YHWH. First the mind then the body, it's not all a loss but we will get there.

Let me give you another perspective of **Is Colour important? And** colour does matter.

Since colour does not matter according to many people then they should perhaps explain black racism. They should explain why in America in many States when a black man goes to buy a house he is charged 8% to 10% on a loan opposed to a white person who is charged half of that amount.

Why in America in the south in redneck areas it says in some barber and bathing stores that blacks are still not allowed?

They should also explain why the pictures of the Messiah and his mother that originally depicted a black woman carrying a black child with fluffy hair suddenly became white?

AND I HEAR YOU SAY COLOUR DOES NOT MATTER!

If colour is not important then why did the South African government have two lifts in the mines one for the black employees and one for the white?

If colour was not important then why ban black Negro men and women marrying white Americans during the slave trade and after as late as 1951 in America in many States?

You see Japheth's actions explain that colour does matter. He has always been fearful of the colour black and fearful that somehow the blacks will take over so he has tried to suppress them.

Notice in Genesis 9:27 Noakh was very careful to put a benediction upon Shem only, he did not include his brother Japheth while many mistake this. Why did he not include a benediction upon Japheth?

> **Gen 9:26-27 (HTHS)** And he said, **Benevolent** is YHWH, the POWER of Shem; and Canaan will become his servant. **27** Elohim will allow **Yapet to be deceived** and he will dwell in the tents of Shem; and Canaan will become his servant.

Noakh actually spoke that Shem will be increased but that YHWH would deceive Yapet and he will possess the houses of Shem (ISRAEL TODAY Occupied by Gentile Khazarian converts from near the Black Sea next to Russia so they are technically Russians).

Noakh knew that Yapet's heart and intentions were not all good this is why he was careful to only speak a positive benediction upon Shem and not on the others. He actually spoke a negative one on Yapet but the gentiles are blind to our scrolls and cannot see that. He wanted all his sons to come under the authority and leadership of the second son Shem.

> **Yashar 7:24** And the garments of skin which Elohim made for Ahdahm and his wife, when they went out of the garden, were given to Cush.

Note the garment of skins that YHWH made for Ahdahm were given to Cush to safeguard but he secretly gave them to his son Nimrood. Note also that it was Shem that Noakh praised which is mentioned by the Torah and he said **Benevolent** is YHWH, the POWER of Shem.

Noakh did not say **Benevolent** is YHWH, the POWER of Yapet because Yapet also was not fully in line in the Torah as were his other two brothers and also there was a clear issue of jealousy on the part of Yapet, which is not only revealed by Noakh's prophecy but also bears out later throughout history to this day. This is why even today blacks are not given credit where credit is due but some other Caucasian person takes credit instead.

Hence why Noakh spoke the way that he did telling us that Yapet will be allowed to be deceived for his part in that he will take over the land of Y'sra'el as he has today and claims he is the chosen while both historically and biblically he has no claim to the land of Y'sra'el and neither are any Ashkenazim or Sephardim chosen. If one is careful to read Genesis 9:27 it is this prophecy that actually put Yapet off from following YHWH and he rebelled even further.

The other corroborating evidence that Yapet was jealous of his brothers is that the book of Yashar mentioned a Yeshivah, a house of learning where Abraham went as a child and it was run by Noakh and Shem so why did Yashar not mention the eldest son Yapet as part of the Yeshivah? It is also known as the Yeshiha of Eber, Jacob studied there.

This is because he like his grandfather Lamekh was not all that interested in the Hebrew faith and had partially backslidden. Lamekh was mentioned as not very strong in the halachot (commandments and ways) of YHWH and unfortunately Yapet followed in his footsteps. Today in the entire world the majority of Atheist countries are those in which Caucasians cohabit while the sons of Shem and sons of Ham have belief in God.

> **Yashar 5:19** And Lamekh the Av of Noakh, died in those days; **yet verily he did not go with all his heart in the halachot of his Av**, and he died in the hundred and ninety-fifth year of the life of Noakh.

We can see why Yapet was influenced more by his grandfather than his father. Lamekh's father Methushelakh was much more forthright and upright he stood with his grandson Noakh to proclaim the Torah truth but Lamekh is never mentioned doing this.

> **Yashar 5:9** And Noakh and Methushelakh spoke all the words of YHWH to the sons of men, day after day, constantly speaking to them.

We can see a picture building where Methushelakh though should be mentioned with his son Lamekh but instead is mentioned with his grandson Noakh which shows one generation of Lamekh missed the boat and were terrible hence why there was so much wickedness, that right-ruling men like Noakh and Methushelakh were sent to teach Torah truths.

> **Yashar 7:34** And when Nimrood was forty years old, at that time there was a war between his brethren and the bnai of Yapet,[37] so that they were in the power of their enemies.

It was this jealousy because YHWH had favoured the Black Nimrood who was the son of Cush and that he had the coats which YHWH had made and was winning battles that Yapet was extremely jealous so his children went to war with Nimrood the Black King. This was the first black and white war if you like in which the whites were utterly defeated. Notice from this war that the Caucasians have ever since been fighting with the sons of Shem and sons of Ham to prove a point but all they have proved is that they are inherently deceptive and double faced.

This means they cannot be trusted as per the nature and name of Yapet, which means high-head, double-face in the ancient Hebrew Hieroglyph script. It's only when Yapet's sons start to walk in the Torah that they remove that bad nature to the good nature inherited from Torah observance to be rightly abiding by the commandments of YHWH. However if Yapet's sons who only do Torah for aesthetics and to look good that is when it shows their hatred for others has not left them.

This is evident in many Israelite Zionist Jews including the late Rabbi Yosef Ovadia of the Shas party who was quite conceited and always going contrary to the Torah. Recently in August 2012 he was praying for the destruction of Iran which is clear evidence that this man has no understanding that within Iran (Phares) are many people of Yahudah. To destroy Iran would be to destroy the children of Y'sra'el because why would YHWH want to establish his throne there if we have none of our people there?

> **Jeremiah 49:38** And I will set my throne in Elam (Iran),

---

[37] It was the jealousy of Yapet that caused this war with Nimrod that why he owned the garments and not Yapet.

and will destroy from there the Sovereign and the princes, says YHWH.

Yashar 7:41 And he placed Terakh the son of Nachor the prince of his host, and he dignified him and elevated him above all his princes.

It was at this decisive battle that Abraham's father Terakh became a prince because he fought the white army on Nimrood's side and defeated the sons of Yapet who were in hostility to Nimrood. Now one can see why the white people at that time started to hate the blacks. Note both Terakh and Nimrood were black while Japheth's sons were white as they were of a paler skin colour. Even though all three sons of Noakh and their children were related but this enmity clearly shows a pattern of jealousy and hatred that has continued to this day.

This is why many Hebrew records of real Y'sra'el were destroyed.

This hopefully should help to explain the jealousy issues we still face today. It is only when the Caucasian races come under the rod of the Messiah that their nature will change and until then we continue to strive to do the right thing according to Torah the everlasting beautiful and magnificent law of YHWH.

Conclusion

This book should leave you in no doubt that Yahushua was indeed black and of African looks with woolly braided hair.

Revelations 1:14-15 His head and his hairs were white like wool, as white as snow; and his eyes were as a flame of fire;**15** And his feet like fine brass, as if they burned in a furnace; and his voice as the sound of many waters.

This description is one of a man of colour. The shocking thing is this, that Elohim reveals himself in the Black race as a black man and why not since he showed the prophet Moses to lead Israel out who was also Black, his beloved servant Dawud who lead one of the most powerful nations in the world Israel was also black and his son the most intelligent king Solomon was Black, Samson a

135

black hero of the Bible who was very strong, all these are different descriptions of YHWH and His might revealed in humanity.

It's an honour for me to know that Yahushua not only took our sins upon Him but was also of Black skin which many racist white people think is inferior and they think their pathetic existence and colour is superior which time will prove is not. The absence or lack of the melanin pigmentation cannot be classed as superior! Academically and medically it is proven that melanin is a very important character in the body and enhances our life and health.

The melanin that the blacks have in their bodies is very good, it protects them from all sorts of diseases that is why God created the first man black. But they the white establishment will not tell you this since Yapet's nature is to continue in his lies.

I encourage you to download and read Melanin the Chemical key to black greatness by Carol Barnes.

A reduction of Melanin in the body leads to the following according to Carol Barnes.

- A reduction in the creation of Knowledge
- A reduction in one's ability to retrieve Memory from storage
- A loss of motivation
- Skin Rashes
- Cancer
- Energy states
- High blood pressure
- Early death

All these from the reduction of Melanin. Cocaine, Marijuana, LSD all these drugs bind to the melanin and can cause irreversible damage hence must never be taken. Other pharmaceutical drug agents can also bind to the Melanin and cause damage that is why some medicines can be so destructive to our health take note the black man out there the Israelite these are all ways to kill you.

[38]The Albino (white man) has numerous body defects due to lack of the genetic to produce Eumelanin. Their Melanocytes, Melanosomes, and mast cells, etc, do not contain the proper catalyst concentration, chemical reactivity and/or electrical charge needed to produce significant levels of Eumelanin is various Melanin centers throughout their bodies. They produce a less effective lower molecular weight melanin called phaeomelanin or pseudomelanin. Therefore, their organs and systems which depend upon Melanin to work effectively do not operate well and may suffer numerous disorders such as rapid aging, cancer, poor physical and mental capabilities, low morals, racism, etc.

This shows you what people have been lying about all along.

Now about the Master Yahushua we need to understand our need is met in this person who meets us down to earth at our level whatever colour or creed we are. What the western people did to the black people during the slavery is well known but also there were good Western folks who helped to eradicate slavery and treat the Blacks with equal amount of humanity. They will be rewarded for their kindness.

However those who took part in embittering the lives of people of colour will one day find themselves on the end of the scales of judgment and everlasting contempt. While the punishment to the Hebrew Israelites was prophesied but were not forever but it did not mean that the ones consciously carrying out these acts get away Scot free, not so, because they will pay the penalty when they are raised and judged to condemnation. The whole of Israel will one day be restored back to the land and the sons of Japheth will be removed who now occupy the land. Today the only people who could be classed as true Hebrews in Israel are the Black people living in Dimona, the Flashas alongside the Sephardic who probably do have a percentage of ancient blood in their veins and the middle-eastern Yahudim.

The majority of Ashkenazim are not of Hebrew extraction and are simply eastern European converts into Judaism. The fact that

---

[38] Page 21 book by Carol Barnes Melanin the Key to black greatness.

they live in prosperity is only because they obeyed the laws of the Torah that our ancestors had not kept them. When the Black Hebrew people start keeping their laws that YHWH gave then the process of restoration will quicken and culminate in them being restored in mind and body. So for all of us it is incumbent upon us all to take this massage of repentance back and cause our people to understand their shortfalls and to start obeying the Torah the beautiful Law of YHWH El Elyon (The Most High). Failure to do this only hastens the coming of the Messiah and the deliverance of our people from the exile and slavery. YHWH still hears our cries and will restore us all back at the appointed time to our Covenants.

Rabbi Simon Altaf Hakohen

Why buy these books?
These books will answer questions you haven't even
thought to ask yet and to polish you on how to serve the
God of Israel.

**We suggest you visit our website to see the following
Titles:**
www.forever-israel.com
Beyth Yahushua – the Son of Tzadok, the Son of Dawud

Would you like to know the identity of Yahushua's family
the man you call Jesus? Did He have brothers and sisters,
did He get married, and are not Rabbis meant to marry?

Is it true if Mary Magdalene was His wife and if not then
what relationship did she have with him?

Who was Nicodemus and what relationship did Yahushua,
have with Nicodemus? Who was the wider family of
Yahushua?

For far too long He has been portrayed as the wandering
man with no belongings and no family and living outside
his home with women offering him money and food. This
picture is both misleading and deceptive.

Do you want to know the powerful family of Yahushua
that was a threat to Rome?

Who were Mark, Luke, and Matthew? Was Luke a gentile
or a Hebrew priest?

What about the genealogy of Luke and Matthew in which
the two fathers of Yahushua mentioned are Heli or Jacob

in Matthew chapter 1:16 and Luke chapter 3:23 respectively?

This book will give you new insights and the rich history of Yahushua.

Islam, Peace or Beast

Have you ever wondered why radical Muslims are blowing up buildings, bombings planes and creating havoc? We illustrate in this book the reality of radical Islam and the end of days that are upon us. Why are our governments reluctant to tell us the truth we uncover many details. Does the Bible reference Middle-Eastern nations or European nations, how many verses can you spot for Europe? Are Muslims just maligned or what we see in Iraq today is what was spoken about in Isaiah 13 and Isaiah 14? The jihad crazed mind, Rev 17, the beast that arose out of the desert, the beheadings now on a TV in front of you myth or reality.

Does the prophet Ezekiel confirm the end is with Islamists or Europeans? Your eyes are about to be opened on a story that began back in Genesis 4000 years ago.

World War III – Unmasking the End-Times Beast

Who is the anti-Messiah, what countries are aligned with him and many of your other questions answered. All revealed in this book. Which might be the ten nations of the anti-Messiah? What did the prophets say on these events? Is the anti-Messiah a Jew? Where is Babylon and the daughter of Babylon in 2015. The true epic battle for Jerusalem. What part will the United States and United Kingdom play in the End of Days. See how accurate Rabbi Simon predicts the coming together of these nations. What are the ships of Kittim, who is Ararat, Minni and

Ashkenaz? Who are the two thirds of people that will be killed?

World War III – Salvation of the Jews
- How will the salvation of the Jews come about, will they convert to Christianity?
- Will the 3rd Temple be built before the coming of the Messiah? Where is the real site of the Third Temple? Analyzed and explained with the correct hermeneutics.
- Will we have a war with Iran and when? Considering the pundits have been wrong since the last 7 years and only Rabbi Simon has been on track up to this time. What signs will absolutely indicate impending war with Iran calculated and revealed.
- When will the Messiah come, what signs should we be looking for, is it on a Jubilee year?
- Will America win the war in Afghanistan? Yes and No answer with details.
- Who is the prince of Ezekiel and why is he making sin sacrifices. Can one call these educational? Read the correct answers...
- Should we support the Jewish Aliyah to Israel?

Rabbi Simon is the only Rabbi to look at the thorny issues that no one has addressed to date while many people mostly run with popular churchy opinions coloured by bad theology by picking and choosing verses in isolation. Is modern Zionism biblical? Is Israel right to take over territories occupied by Palestinians today? Should people be selling up homes to go and live in Israel? All these thorny questions and even more answered in this book the sequel to the popular prophecy book World War III - Unmasking the End-Times Beast.

Dear Muslim – Meet YHWH the Elohim of Abraham
Truth explained, best seller step by step detailing and
unveiling Islam! This book is designed for that friend, son
or daughter who is about to convert into Islam but needs
to read this first. This is the <u>one</u> stop to saving their soul.
Don't procrastinate, get it today so that they may see what
is the truth before they cause themselves to be confounded
and duped into something totally not true.

The Feasts of YHWH, the Elohim of Israel
Have you ever asked why the feasts were given to Israel as
a people? What is the meaning of the festivals and what
about their purpose which is all explained in this detailed
book that delves into this? Why are we to obey the feasts
forever and if we do not then we could potentially lose our
place in the kingdom entry! Well no one said that before
but now you will see and experience an exhilarating
experience of knowing what it is like to be there. How does
it feel to be up all night to celebrate the festival of Shavuot
(Pentecost), what does it mean and many other details.

Testament of Abraham
Now it's time to hear Abraham's story from his own mouth
what happened, how did he become God's friend. What
other missing information that we are not told about is
made available. Without Abraham there will be no Judaism,
no Islam and no Christianity. He is the pivotal point upon
which all three religious text claim right but who does
Abraham really belong to?

What is Truth?
Have you wondered what truth is and how we measure it?
How do we arrive at the conclusion that what you have is

truth? How do you know that the religion you have been following for so many years is the original faith? Can we examine Atheism and say why it is or is not true. We examine these things.

Yeshua or Isa
If you want to witness to your Muslim friends or relatives about the truth of Yahushua and the Holy Bible, this is a must have book.

Hidden Truths Hebraic Scrolls Tanak 7th Edition
The Bible more myths busted. Packed absolutely full of information - no Hebrew roots Bible even comes close this is guaranteed and these scrolls are the difference between night and day, see for yourself!!! The politically incorrect guide to the Elohim of Israel and the real chosen people of YHWH. Are you willing to listen to what YHWH has said about our world and how He is going to restore all things back including His real chosen people hidden to this day? Many texts uncovered and explained in great details accurately and many corrections made to the many faulty translations out there making this a real eye-opener text.

→ Was Chava (Eve) the only woman in the garden? We reveal a deep held secret.
→ Where did the demons come from?
→ Ezekiel refers to some of Israel's evil deeds in Egypt explicitly uncovered which are glossed over in the King James Version.
→ Who are the Real Hebrews of the Bible, which people does the land of Y'sra'el really belong to? Time to do away with the deception.

- ➜ Did Abraham keep the Sabbath? We show you when and where.
- ➜ But I thought Keturah was Hagar, another error of Judaism corrected.
- ➜ But I thought Keturah was married to Abraham after Sarah's death, no not really. A very bad textual translation.
- ➜ Who was Balaam, a profit for cash as are many pastors and Bishops today doing the same thing running and chasing after the Almighty dollar?
- ➜ Who were Abraham's ancestors, Africa or Europeans?
- ➜ Why did Isaac marry at forty years of age, what happened to his first wife? Rebecca was not his only wife, an error and ignorance of Christendom exposed?
- ➜ Where is Noah's ark likely to be? Not Ararat in Turkey or Iran another error.
- ➜ Who are the four wives of Abraham and who is the real firstborn? Not Ishmael and not even Isaac. Was Isaac his only begotten son another error?
- ➜ All the modification of modern Judaism of the scribes has been undone to give you what was the real text including the original conversation of the Serpent with Chava (Gen 3) unedited plus Abraham's conversation unedited at last in Genesis 18.

The legendary Rabbi Simon Altaf Hakohen guarantees that this will teach you to take the best out there and open their eyes in prophecy, historical argument and theology. He will personally mentor you through the texts of the Torah, the prophets. Does any Bible seller offer this extent of training?

We do. And Rabbi Simon is available at the end of an e-mail or just a telephone call away for questions that you have all this time.

Sefer Yashar (The Book of Jasher)

The book of Yashar has been translated from the original sources and with added commentary, corrected names of Elohim with the sacred names and with other missing text from the Hebrew. This will add to the gaps in your knowledge from the book of Genesis such as the following:
- What did the wicked do before the flood?
- Who were Abraham's African ancestors?
- Did Abraham have two wives?
- What relationship did Abraham have with Eli'ezer?
- Did Isaac wait forty years to be married?
- Why did Sarah die so suddenly?
- Did Moses marry in Egypt?
- Moses, what colour? White or Black.
- Many other questions now answered.

Seferim Chanoch (The Books of Enoch)

The books of Enoch details the fall, the names of the angels, what happened in the beginning and what was the result of those fallen angels. Where are they now and what will happen to them. He also reveals the birth of Noach and some very important details around this about the African ancestry of the patriarchs. And many other important details to complete your knowledge.

Yahushua, The Black Messiah

Have you been lied to about the true identity of Yahushua? Have you been shown pictures of the idolatrous Borgia Cesare and may have believed that this Caucasian hybrid was Yahushua. What ethnicity was Yahushua and what race of people did He belong to? Is it important that we know His ethnicity? What colour was Moses, King David and King Solomon? We examine and look at the massive fraud perpetrated upon the western nations by their leaders to hide the real identity of the true Hebrew Israelite people and race which are being restored in these Last Days. Would you like to know because it affects your eternity and His true message then get this book now.

Hebrew Wisdom – Kabbalah in the Brit Ha Chadasha
The book's purpose is to illustrate basic principles of Kabbalah and to reveal some of the Kabbalah symbolisms. We look at the Sefirots what they mean and how they apply to some of the teachings. We also look at the first chapter in Genesis and examine some of the symbols there. We examine the name of Elohim in Exodus 3:14 and see what it means.

The Apocrypha (With Pirke Avot 'Ethics of The Fathers')
Read the fifteen books of the Apocrypha to get an understanding of the events both of the exile and of Israel's early history. Read Ethics of the Fathers to understand rabbinic wisdom and some important elements of the story of Genesis. The tests, the trials and the miracles of the Temples. Without these books the story in the bible is incomplete and has gaps which these books will fill up and give you a more complete understanding.

Forever-israel Siddur transliterated Hebrew with English (Daily life prayers 7th Edition)
Many times we wonder what prayers should we do when we go to bed, when we leave our home in the morning and how do we pray daily? What prayer should I do if I have a ritual bath? What prayer is for affixing a Mezuzah? Each

year you wonder how to do the Passover Aggadah and what is the procedure. This book also covers women's niddah laws to give you understanding into women's ritual purity. Unlike other prayer books Rabbi Simon Altaf actually bothers to explain small details that are important and often ignored. This is one book you should not be without. The festival readings and the 72 names of God are included in the text.

World War III, The Second Exodus, Y'sra'el's return journey home

How will the genetic Hebrews be taken back to the land? Are the present day Jews in Y'sra'el of ancient stock? Is there any prophecy of foreigners invading Y'sra'el and inhabiting the land? How will Elohim have war with Amalek and wipe them out and who is Amalek today? Why is the Church so confused about bible prophecy?
How will the end come and why is the world hiding the identity of the true Y'sra'elites? Will there be a rapture or marching back on foot? What happens if we die in our exile? And many more questions answered. The time has come to expose the errors of others.

What Else Have They Kept From Us?

This book is as the result of an e-mail conversation with a lady who asked me some questions and one of her questions upon my answer was "What else have they kept from us?" This was the question that led to this book because instead of answering people with small sections of answers I decided the time had come that a book had to be written to answer and address everything as it happened from the start to the end so that many may see that the deception is real and it's a deep cunning deception which

147

starts from your TV screens, in your newspapers followed by wherever you go in your daily life.

How would a person know that they are being deceived if they do not know what to look for? Its like a Ten Pound note well if you saw the original then you have something to compare the false note with but what if you were never presented with the original and always had the fake in your pocket then you will likely think the fake is real and this is how it is with Christianity today that is simply mixing paganism with truth. A false Ten pound note or a bad tender which will give you no value when you redeem it as I uncover it in the pages of this book. Who was Yahushua, the real Hebrews and Israel.

Patriarchal Marriage, Y'sra'el's Right-Ruling Way of Life, Methods and Practice

How did the Y'sra'elites live? What form of marriage did they practice and how did they practice it? This book is about to show you what was God's design from the beginning and how the Y'sra'elites lived within God's required parameters. Today these things appear mythological but here we show you the methods and ways of how this lifestyle was practiced and is being restored in these last days, while the much touted gentile monogamy is wrecking lives destroying families and society around us. How many marriages are breaking down as a result of the wrong model and how many children are living fatherless lives, while women live husbandless and unfulfilled lives. This book will show you why the Greek and Roman monogamy model with a husband and a wife and a bit on the side does not work. While Elohim's model of plural marriage is an everlasting model that not only works but saves many children from losing their father's and women from losing good husbands.

The Scroll of Yahubel (Jubilees)
The information that is missing in the Torah has been put in here to aid us in understanding the book of Genesis more. There are gaps in Genesis with what happened with Noakh? What was going on in Moses's time? This scroll allows us to piece together that information that is so important for our understanding. True names edition with many corrections made.

Who am I?
A Children's book to help the black Hebrew children with identity and direction in life. Many Hebrew children while looking for identity easily stray. While they search for love they end up in gangs to prove themselves and search for that missing something. When they do not find love in their homes due to broken homes often venturing out with devastating consequences, getting involved in criminal activities to prove themselves ruining their lives. This book's purpose is to help these children and even adults find themselves to teach them who they are and to find sound direction in life to secure you to the God of our ancestors where you belong. This will help change many lives.

Hidden Truths Hebraic Scrolls Compendium Guide
Chumash Torah - For those who have the Hidden-Truths Hebraic Scrolls this is a must buy to give you a deeper understanding under the text and its meaning where the footnotes are expounded upon further in various books of the scrolls. To learn the secrets of the Torah. All the

Parshas expounded for further understanding. It also contains all the parsha notes.

Hebrew Characters, The Power to have prayers answered

Have you ever tried praying and find that either your prayers take very long time to answer or they don't get answered at all? In frustration you ask other friends to pray for you in hope that you may get an answer from God soon. I have given considerable thought about the condition of our people and how many languish in poverty, in situations where they seek for help because they are given false dogmas, put in religious bondage and slavery of the mind and heart.

Many times they make their own lives harder because they have spent so much time in the nations that they just want to live like the gentiles and not Hebrew as they are unaware how to benefit themselves that await them. I know it can be a lonely road at times. Our Abbah in the heavens feels our pain while we live in exile He sends the Shekinah to be with us. He longs for us to return back to the contracts that we may receive all the increases and benefits that are only meant for us.

However we pass our life by with this that and the other person who gives us no joy but we think maybe if we carry on suffering things will change for the better but things NEVER change. This book was written to help for a time such as this to better the lives of our people. To empower them with the right petitions to give them benefits and increases in employment, love, marriage and sickness. This will help you break the spells of witchcraft, dealing with jealous people around you and personal anger issues. This will help you deal with demonic presences in your homes.

This will show you how to receive a timely answer to all your prayers. I have used these methods for my students all over the world which have proven successful for them and have greatly benefited them.

It takes many generations for a right-ruling priest to be born in our generations. How many generations our people have suffered the scourge of the curses for not obeying the Torah? Many are still suffering. The Most High is going to raise his priests one by one until we get our restoration complete. Rabbi Simon is of the priestly family born to help his people.

The Kohen is meant to be a benefit to the people of Y'sra'el and is one of the person's that has been given the authority to stand between the heavenly court and the earthly realm. Christian clergy has been lying to you for so long that you don't know what is good for you anymore. The Melekzadek priest's job is not to stand between the heaven and earth as you have been wrongly taught, his job is to be a King and serve justice on the earth with the Torah. While the Christian clergy teaches everyone can be a Melekzadek this is not the truth. Only the Kings of Israel can right hold that title, it's not for anyone else.

There is only one everlasting priesthood and that is the Lewitical one. This book has been written by a Lewitical priest of Beyth of Tzadok, its time you reap the benefits so decide wisely. Even if you are a gentile looking to become part of Israel by conversion the opportunity is open to you to obey the Torah and join us.

151

I want you all to benefit and to receive what rightly belongs to you.

I could have sold this book for $100 a piece because everything in this manual would forever change your life once you put it in practice but I decided not to do that as my purpose was to help my people and not hinder them, now the rest is up to you if you want to take the next step.

Now that I know I am a Hebrew

You don't just wake up one day and say You are a Hebrew. Being Hebrew brings many processes that need to be completed before you are finally cleaned up as the Abbah desires to fulfil your responsibilities. This book is in the hope to help many of our people who are Hebrews and desiring the change to rid them of idolatry and clean up to present to the Abbah a sacrifice with sweet aroma so that they may serve Him faithfully according to His desire! Are you willing to make the sacrifices required to follow the God of Israel?

Religious Confusion and the Everlasting Path to the Torah

Everyone claims their religion is the truth or you will go to hell. The Torah makes only one claim that God is interested in our world affairs.

All those that are confused about which religion to follow there is only one voice of God and that voice is found in the Torah of Moses. For your eternal rest and peace in your life choose the Torah. This book helps you to make the wise choice to help your life. Everything around you is compromised and the entire man made religions claim to truth is nothing but smokes and mirrors to cheat people

out of their eternal destiny. Turn back to the Torah to find
your eternal future and hope.

To Purchase more books for study and reference

The Hidden Truths Hebraic Scrolls Tanak or Complete Bible can
be ordered at the URL below. www.forever-israel.com. Note the
excellent translation of bible which reflects our mission to Africa
and to Israel worldwide and the true genetic Hebrews mentioned in
the bible who live in the western word such as in Europe,
Americas and in the Caribbean islands including many other
countries like Brazil, India, Iran and Pakistan.

Why buy these books?
These books will answer questions you haven't even thought to ask
yet and to polish you on how to serve the God of Israel.
Beyth Yahushua – the Son of Tzadok, the Son of Dawud
Islam, Peace or Beast
World War III – Unmasking the End-Times Beast
World War III – Salvation of the Jews
Dear Muslim – Meet YHWH the Elohim of Abraham
The Feasts of YHWH, the Elohim of Israel
Testament of Abraham
What is Truth?
Hidden Truths Hebraic Scrolls Tanak 7th Edition
Hidden Truths Hebraic Scrolls Torah
Hidden Truths Hebraic Scrolls Brit Ha Chadasha (NT)
Hidden Truths Hebraic Scrolls Study Bible Complete
The Torah Chumash is a commentary in addition to the
popular translation of the Hidden Truths Hebraic Scrolls
translated by Rabbi Simon Altaf revealing some deep secrets
with all the Parshas
Sefer Yashar (The Book of Jasher)
Seferim Chanoch (The Books of Enoch)
Yahushua, The Black Messiah

Hebrew Wisdom – Kabbalah
The Apocrypha (With Pirke Avot Ethics of The Fathers)
Forever-israel Siddur transliterated Hebrew with English
(Daily life prayers 7th Edition)
World War III, The Second Exodus, Y'sra'el's return journey
home
What Else Have They Kept From Us?
Patriarchal Marriage, Y'sra'el's Right-Ruling Way of Life,
Methods and Practice
The Scroll of Yahubel (Jubilees)
Who am I?
Hebrew Characters, The Power to have prayers answered
Now that I know I am a Hebrew
Religious Confusion and the Everlasting Path to the Torah

37492922R00086

Made in the USA
Middletown, DE
27 February 2019